I Thought I Heard
A Rustling

A Play

Alan Plater

A SAMUEL FRENCH ACTING EDITION

**SAMUEL
FRENCH**

FOUNDED 1830

SAMUELFRENCH-LONDON.CO.UK
SAMUELFRENCH.COM

FOR AMATEUR PRODUCTION ENQUIRIES

UNITED KINGDOM AND WORLD
EXCLUDING NORTH AMERICA
plays@SamuelFrench-London.co.uk
020 7255 4302/01

Each title is subject to availability from Samuel French,

depending upon country of performance.

I THOUGHT I HEARD A RUSTLING

First performed at the Theatre Royal, Stratford East, on 30th January 1991, with the following cast:

Bill Robson	Paul Copley
Ellen Scott	Annette Crosbie
Gerald Nutley	Robert Daws
Councillor Graham	Kate Williams
Bernard	Jake Wood

The play directed by **Philip Hedley**
Designed by **Jenny Tiramani**

The action of the play takes place in the back room of a small branch library on the edge of London, with two excursions to a room in the Civic Centre Annexe

ACT I   SCENE 1   The Civic Centre Annexe. Morning
           SCENE 2   The library. Morning
           SCENE 3   The library. A week later. Morning

ACT II   SCENE 1   The library. A couple of hours later. Afternoon
           SCENE 2   The Civic Centre Annexe. Morning
           SCENE 3   The library. A month later. Morning

Time—the present

ACT I

A room in the Civic Centre Annexe. Morning

The room is being used for a press conference, organized by a small Local Authority somewhere on the edges of London. Three stacking chairs are set in front of a small screen bearing the authority's logo. The logo comprises two or three capital letters so distorted it is impossible to tell what they are, together with the slogan: "WORKING FOR YOU"

Three people walk on, looking a little self-conscious, and sit down on the chairs

They are: Councillor Graham, who takes the centre chair. She is a Liberal-Democrat person who took up politics when her kids left school, in preference to an Open University degree. It might have been the wrong choice. To one side of her sits Ellen, a senior librarian who has devoted her working life to the care of books. She is an endangered species. To the other side sits Bill, a down-to-earth Geordie. He's in his mid-thirties: a generation younger than Ellen, half a generation younger than Graham

Graham scans the room. She's a little disappointed with what she sees

Graham Do you think we should start?
Ellen Well, we are five minutes late already.
Graham I don't understand. We circulated all the Nationals. (*She turns to Bill*) *Are you ready?*
Bill Ready when you are, pet.

Graham smiles, but not happily. She isn't comfortable being addressed as "pet"

Graham Good. (*She turns to the audience*)

Hereabouts we become aware of Nutley sitting in the front row. He's a keen-eyed, earnest young man, occupying the fringes of some brand of highly personal zealotry

Good-morning. My name is Councillor Graham. Deputy-Co-Chair-Person of the Libraries Sub-Committee. Welcome to the Civic Centre Annexe. The purpose of this press conference is to welcome our new writer-in-residence, Mr William Robinson.
Bill Robson.
Graham I'm sorry?

Bill I think you'll find, on closer examination, that my name's Robson. Bill Robson.

Graham checks her copy of the press release

Graham I do beg your pardon.

Bill Granted.

Graham For the next three months, Mr Robson will be resident at our Eastwood Road branch, and his experience and expertise will be available to writers and would-be writers in the local community. Mrs Scott . . . (*a half-turn to Ellen*) . . . is in charge of the branch. I don't know whether there is anything you would like to say about the appointment, Mrs Scott . . . ?

Ellen Let me see, what would I like to say? Yes. I would like to say that this will be the first time we have had a writer-in-residence in residence and we shall do all we can to make Mr Robson comfortable. Even though I have no idea where we're going to put him. (*With a smile at Bill. She's scoring political points about shortage of space*)

Graham (*taking the point*) We are familiar with Mrs Scott's memos about the shortage of space at our Eastwood Road branch and I would like to give my personal assurance as Deputy-Co-Chair-Person of the Libraries Sub-Committee that we are taking the matter on board as an urgent matter of the highest priority. (*Another cool smile from Graham before she turns to the audience once more*) I apologize for that little lurch into internal politics. Meanwhile, back at the agenda . . . (*her best effort at a joke*) . . . I have to place on record my disappointment at the dismal response from the national and local press and media but we are, nonetheless, grateful to you, sir, for being with us this morning. You are . . . ?

Nutley stands up, without too much conviction

Nutley Nutley.

Graham Mr Nutley. Thank you for being with us. Is there anything you would like to ask any of us?

Nutley I have one or two questions, yes. First of all——

Graham Would you like to identify which newspaper you represent? It's a Council rule, I'm afraid. Boring old bureaucracy. The Liberal-Democrats are pledged to get rid of it, but with a hung Council we get the worst of all worlds.

Nutley I'm a free-lance.

Graham Ah. (*She flips through her file without much hope of finding anything relevant*) I'm not sure what our standing orders have to say about free-lance journalists.

Ellen (*to the rescue*) Mr Nutley is an old friend of the Eastwood Road branch. I'm sure anything you tell him will be treated with total respect and responsibility.

Graham Thank you, Mrs Scott. (*She's off the hook and turns again to Nutley*) Please ask your questions, Mr Nutley.

Nutley Is it true there's been a big row in the Council about Mr Robson's appointment?

Graham A medium-sized row.

Bill But they don't even know me.

Graham The row was about the principle of the thing.

Bill If there's a principle of the thing, you're guaranteed a row.

Nutley If I may ask . . . how big is a medium-sized row?

Graham Bigger than the row about the purchase of South African tinned grapefruit. Smaller than the row about privatizing our garbage.

Bill If *I* may ask . . . what principle? What thing?

Graham The Tories think a writer-in-residence is a sinful waste of public money. The Socialists think it's a creative use of public money.

Nutley And the Liberal-Democrat view?

Graham (*after hesitating*) It seemed to us that the truth lay somewhere between the two extremes.

Bill Well spotted.

Nutley But presumably the Liberal-Democrats voted in favour?

Graham Once we discovered the money was not coming from the rates, but was a grant from the regional arts association. It isn't ratepayers' money at all, except in a very broad, almost metaphysical sense. (*And she attempts another joke*) We quite like spending public money, providing it isn't ours.

Bill It's like getting drunk when somebody else is paying.

Which doesn't amuse Graham. Ellen stifles a yawn

Graham If there are no more questions——

Nutley (*breaking in*) I have a question for Mr Robson.

Bill Ready when you are, bonny lad.

Nutley What exactly do you write?

Bill I'm a poet. I think you'll find it's down there in the press release. A poet. That's what I am.

Nutley Have you published any of your work?

Bill Why no. It's not that easy, being a poet, you know. Like, there's no overwhelming public demand for poetry. Especially where I come from.

Ellen (*gently supporting*) Mr Robson isn't a local man.

Nutley So I . . . suspected.

Ellen (*to Graham*) Would it be in order if I sketched in the background, Madam Deputy-Co-Chair? Briefly.

Graham Why not? I can't speak for the other two parties but we believe in open government.

Ellen Mr Robson is, or strictly speaking *was* a coal-miner. He came South during the strike to raise money for the union.

Bill I'm from the North-East, you see. County Durham.

Ellen And when the strike was over——

Bill The scabs began to sing . . . (*He turns quickly, apologetically, to Graham*) Sorry, Madam Deputy-Co-Chair. These things come into my head. It's to do with being a poet, I daresay.

Graham I daresay.

Ellen (*gently re-phrasing*) *After* the strike, Mr Robson's pit was closed and he was made redundant.

Bill I stayed here in the South. Trying to find work.

Nutley And make your way as a poet and writer?

Bill You've hit the nail right on the nose, bonny lad.

Graham If there are no more questions——

Nutley (*breaking in*) I have another question.

Graham Could you keep it moderately brief, Mr Nutley? I have a Cemeteries Sub-Committee in a few minutes . . .

Nutley It's a moderately brief question.

Graham Good.

Nutley All applicants for the post of writer-in-residence were asked to submit examples of their work. Since you haven't published anything, I simply wondered what you submitted, Mr Robson?

Bill Since I haven't published anything, I submitted some unpublished work. (*He digs into a cardboard folder*) In an exercise book. (*From the folder he produces the exercise book*) This exercise book. My collected works.

Nutley Is there any possibility that interested members of the public might have a chance to read your collected works?

Graham The Libraries Sub-Committee hopes to publish some of Mr Robson's work.

Ellen If some grant aid is available . . .

Graham Or business sponsorship . . .

Bill We'll probably approach bookmakers and breweries first. The Newcastle Brown Collected Works of Bill Robson. That sounds canny. (*He stands up*) Now if there are no more questions, time's getting on and I should really be in residence.

A lighting change. A little North-Eastern music over: say a nice quote from "Dance To Thi Daddy". Minimal set change. The display screen turns around to become part of the new set, and the chairs remain. Swiftly and painlessly we move on to:

SCENE 2

The small back room behind the Eastwood Road branch of the public library. Morning

The room combines the functions of office, tea-room, storeroom and is, naturally enough, stacked high and wide with books. There's a door leading to the lending library and we might, from time to time, catch a hint of activity in that area. On a table or bench stand a computer keyboard and screen and adjacent to that, a small wheeled trolley laden with books

Ellen sits at the keyboard, tapping away with a professional dedication of a desultory nature. Bill wanders around, exploring

Bill How long have you worked here?

Ellen Approximately ... one thousand, two hundred and seventy-three years.

Bill opens the odd cupboard or drawer. He's a straight-ahead nosy parker

Bill How are you settling in?

Ellen I've almost overcome my initial shyness.

Bill wanders across to the doorway leading to the lending library

Bill Is that the library through there?

Ellen The room with all the books on shelves. Yes, that's the library. Sometimes people come in off the street and borrow them. They have special tickets for the purpose.

Bill Library tickets.

Ellen Got it in one.

Bill You learn to think quickly working at the coal face.

Ellen If there are no more questions ...

Bill I've got lots more questions ...

Ellen In that case, we'll have a tea break. (*She gets up*)

Bill We've only just clocked in.

Ellen Most days I start with a tea break. It saves time later.

Bill I thought it was only the feckless working classes that filled their time with tea breaks.

Ellen That's a story put about by the feckless middle classes. (*She takes a kettle from its appointed place*)

Ellen exits to fill the kettle in a small cloakroom off stage, returns, plugs it in and switches it on

While she does so, Bill looks at her computer keyboard

Watch this. Mark it well. If we're going to share this room, you'll have to take your turn making the tea.

Bill I'm very good at making tea.

Ellen Good. (*She sits down and waits for the kettle*) Ask your questions.

Bill All right. Question number one. What the hell am I supposed to do all day?

Ellen You do whatever a writer-in-residence normally does.

Bill But I've never been one before.

Ellen You make your skill and expertise available to the community.

Bill They're not exactly flocking in, are they?

Ellen Perhaps they will, once your reputation spreads.

Bill So, while I'm waiting for the people to flock in, what the hell do I do all day?

Ellen You could sit in your small corner and write something.

Bill Write something?

Ellen You're a poet. You said so at the press conference. Buy another exercise book. Fill it with poems.

Bill That's all very well, but I don't really see the point.

Ellen A poet who doesn't see the point in writing poems?

Bill That's right.

Ellen Isn't that like being a coal-miner who doesn't see any point in digging for coal?

Bill I never did see any point in hewing coal.

Ellen I don't know. Coal gives us light and heat. I quite enjoy both, in their proper place.

The kettle boils hereabouts. Ellen makes the tea and pours it during this sequence

Bill I've got nothing against light and heat. I've got nothing against coal. But I never saw any point in me digging it out of the ground. It was dark and dirty and dangerous. I'm very happy for somebody else to dig it out for me. And it's the same with poetry. I mean, this is only a little library, isn't it? But you've got stacks of poetry in there. And I bet there's stacks more at head office. And they're all canny lads like Shakespeare and Wordsworth and Shelley and Blake. I'm not fit to lace their boots. So why bother trying?

Ellen Why indeed? I enjoyed reading your slim volume. (*She delves into her shopping bag. She brings out Bill's exercise book full of poems: the slim volume that got him the job. She opens the book*) The collected poems of William Robson.

Bill I'm embarrassed to even look at them.

Ellen And I know why you're embarrassed.

Bill Do you?

Ellen You stole them, didn't you?

Bill Yes. (*He looks sharply at her*) How do you know?

Ellen I read them.

Pause

Bill Is that all?

Ellen Yes.

Bill All you did was read them? And you could tell, just by reading them, they were all knocked off, like?

Ellen It's the price I pay for being an educated woman.

Bill That's incredible. I mean, how did you do it? How could you tell?

Ellen Well, for a start, there were twenty poems, written in twenty different styles.

Bill Oh, I see. You reckon that was a mistake?

Ellen I reckon that was a mistake.

Bill You see, I thought if I stole them all from the same feller, like Tennyson or Keats, only not as famous as them, there'd be more chance of getting found out. That's why I played the field. And I tried to pick like obscure people.

Ellen Not all that obscure.

Bill No?

Ellen I can give you half a dozen names at least. (*She leafs through the book*) That's Bertolt Brecht . . . that's Pablo Neruda . . . that's Langston Hughes . . . where did you find them? A book of Socialist verse?

Bill Something of the sort.

Ellen And there's a poem by Roger McGough, translated from Liverpool into Geordie . . .

Bill Yes, I tried to improve it a bit. (*He is totally relaxed about Ellen's discovery*)

Ellen You don't seem very worried.

Bill What is there to worry about?

Ellen Getting the job under false pretences? Isn't that a criminal offence?

Bill Maybes. But it's not *much* of a criminal offence.

Ellen Why did you do it?

Bill I needed the job.

Ellen But why *this* job? There are other jobs.

Bill I've tried other jobs. Listen, pet. I get a hundred pounds a week for doing this, and so far it's a doddle. The only other time I got a hundred pounds a week since I left the pit was washing up at an Indian curry house. And even then, I had to take my overtime in chicken vindaloo. The system can't cope with that for very long.

Ellen Vindaloo, yes, I can understand. But I still don't approve.

Bill What don't you approve of? I told a bit of a lie, that's all.

Ellen Somewhere out there's probably a *real* writer who could have done the job properly.

Bill Somebody with skill and expertise?

Ellen Yes, and talent, and dedication, and integrity——

Bill (*breaking in*) Well there might be some young genius lying bleeding and neglected in the gutter, but he didn't make the short-list, that's all I can say.

Ellen Who *did* make the short-list?

Bill There was a sensitive and dedicated little lass that wanted to bring the theatre to the masses. Like out on the streets. But she got a chance to write for "EastEnders". So that only left me and a chinless youth who kept saying: (*posh voice*) "I have this irresistible urge to express myself." I didn't bother with any of that.

Ellen So it was between you and the chinless youth?

Bill That's right, pet.

Ellen Please don't call me pet. I am not a hamster.

Bill Ay, I can tell you're not a hamster.

Ellen Who interviewed you?

Bill Councillor Graham, Deputy-Co-Chair-Person of the Libraries Sub-Committee, representing the Liberal-Democrats. Councillor Baxter, Deputy-Co-Chair-Person of the Libraries Sub-Committee . . .

Ellen Representing the Labour Party.

Bill You know Councillor Baxter?

Ellen I know Councillor Baxter. He's a university lecturer.

Bill But he'd really like to be common as muck, like I am. Asked me a lot of questions about whippet-racing among the miners.

Ellen And who was representing the Conservative Pary?

Bill That should have been Councillor Bradley-hyphen-Willis, the other Co-Deputy-Chair-Person but he didn't turn up, on account of there being a run on his shares in the City. I think the chinless youth that wanted to express himself was the Tory Party runner, so the poor kid didn't really stand a chance on the day.

Ellen And you triumphed with your street credibility.

Bill Why ay, man.

Ellen I am not a man.

Bill Sorry. Not a man. Not a hamster.

Ellen But as a result of this all-party shambles of a committee, you were appointed writer-in-residence to this library.

Bill It was dead easy. You get a Labour man that wishes he was working class and isn't. And he meets a real live pitman that never crossed a picket line in his life. It's no contest.

Ellen How did you cope with Councillor Graham of the Liberal-Democrats?

Bill Used my loaf. Made sure I said one or two reasonable and balanced things. You know, on the one hand this, on the other hand that. It doesn't much matter what you're talking about as long as there's two sides to it.

Ellen Not only dishonest and deceitful but skilful with it.

Bill I've always been told I interview well.

Ellen It's just that you can't do anything.

Bill Apart from hewing coal.

Ellen Apart from hewing coal.

Bill And they closed the pit. Anyways, most people can't do anything. They just pretend they can.

Ellen I don't pretend.

Bill You don't?

Ellen If there was a Eurovision Librarian Contest, I'd be in the first three every time.

Bill I'll believe you. I'm not sure it's worth the effort, mind——

Ellen (*breaking in, sharp*) Not worth the effort!

Bill I mean, the public isn't exactly flocking in. There's no mad rush of people wanting to improve their minds. (*He positions himself so he can see through the door into the lending library, and thus confirm it's deserted*) Look at it. It's like a street in Sunderland when the pubs are open.

Ellen I don't mind that you're illiterate, Mr Robson. I don't mind that you're an imposter. I don't mind that you cheated your way past a committee of local politicians who probably cheated their way on to the committee in the first place. But don't flaunt your ignorance and gloss it over with proletarian charm. It won't work on me.

Bill I'll make a note. Go easy on the proletarian charm.

Ellen You're doing it again already.

Bill Sorry.

Ellen And the other thing you mustn't do while you're working here . . . never do the dirty on books, on writers, on literature, on the English language, on the word.

Bill (*gently*) In the beginning was the word?

Ellen Exactly. (*She crosses to the window and looks out*) I look out of the window and I see a supermarket and a multi-storey car-park, and an old chapel waiting for the demolition men. They'll knock it down to make room for more supermarket and more multi-storey car-park. What does that prove about civilization, Mr Robson?

Bill It's up the Swanee.

Ellen But on the other hand——

Bill (*breaking in*) On the other hand? Do you vote for the Liberal-Democrats?

Ellen (*ignoring him*) On the other hand, civilization does make progress. About one inch every century. Once upon a time I would have looked out of this window and seen public executions and sewage flowing down the street.

Bill You can still see all them things in Sunderland.

Ellen Shut up and listen!

Bill (*respectfully*) Listening.

Ellen The reason civilization moves forward one inch every century is this ... (*she picks up a book from the rack she's working from*) ... or this ... or this ... or this ... (*picking up a series of books*) ... and somebody reads something ... an idea leaps from the page and into the mind ... a moment of truth ... and the idea leaps from the mind and out on to the streets ...

Bill But there's millions of books and millions of people. Getting the right person to read the right book so that something like that happens ... the odds don't bear thinking about.

Ellen It's all we've got. The word.

Bill In the beginning.

Ellen And the middle and the end.

Pause

Don't do the dirty on the word, Mr Robson.

Bill I'll ... try to remember. (*He sees somebody come into the lending library*) You've got a customer.

Ellen Have I? (*She heads towards the door*)

Bill (*as Ellen passes him*) Some feller popped in for the moment of truth. In paperback.

Ellen Bollocks to you, Mr Robson.

She exits

He's a little startled by her reaction, and sits down in his designated chair. He pulls a copy of "The Sporting Life" from his pocket and is starting to browse through today's runners and riders when ...

Ellen returns

Not a customer for me. A customer for you. An aspiring writer wishing to avail himself of your skill, expertise and wisdom. (*Then, in a good parody of his accent*) A moment of truth, pet.

Nutley enters. He's carrying a cardboard box of the sort that normally contains five reams of A4 typing paper

Nutley Good-morning, Mr Robson.

Bill Good-morning. (*He recognizes Nutley*) We've met before. You were at the press conference.

Ellen Mr Nutley *was* the press conference.

Nutley I hope you don't mind my turning up without an appointment but I happened to be in the area and——

Bill (*breaking in*) What? Demolishing the old chapel?

Nutley I'm sorry?

Bill And you thought you'd put the system to the test. (*He pulls up the spare chair*) Take a seat. We keep this one warm, specially for aspiring writers.

Nutley Thank you.

Ellen sits down at her keyboard. She is typing details of the books on the rack into the machine

Ellen You'll forgive me if I get on with my work? I'll try not to make a fuss.

Bill Treat the place as if it was your own, hinny.

Ellen (*mouthing*) Hinny. (*She is not amused. Louder*) It'll be very exciting to hear two creative minds at work.

Bill I daresay. (*He sits down, and turns to Nutley, very brisk and business-like*) Now, Mr Nutley, what can we do for you?

Nutley I'm hoping you can help me with my novel.

Bill We'll certainly try. Is this a novel you've written? Or a novel you're going to write? Or one you've written and torn up? We get all sorts in here, you know.

Nutley It's really work in progress.

Bill I thought you were a newspaper man?

Nutley That's a temporary situation. Until I break through as a proper, grown-up novelist.

Bill Joined-up writing. All that.

Nutley That's one way of expressing it.

Ellen Proletarian charm.

Nutley I'm sorry?

Ellen It's a book title. (*She indicates her keyboard*) I'm putting all the library's records on to computer. It helps if I talk to myself every sixty seconds. Approximately.

Nutley I see. (*He doesn't really but what the hell*)

Bill You'd better tell me about your work in progress, Mr Nutley.

Nutley It's a trilogy.

Bill Is it now? (*He's a little uncertain what the word means*)

Nutley I'm afraid so.

Bill (*boldy guessing*) That must make it a bit harder than an ordinary book.

Nutley You can say that again.

Bill Thanks for the invitation but I won't bother. It's a very old joke.

Nutley (*baffled but continuing*) I suppose in terms of pure mathematics it's three times as hard as writing one book.

Bill (*working it out*) On account of it being, more or less, three books?

Nutley Exactly.

Bill Definitely.

Ellen With one bound he was free.

They look at her. She holds up a book

Victorian melodrama. Nobody reads it now.

Bill (*resuming his interview*) So how are you getting on with er ... your trilogy?

Nutley I've written two-thirds of it.

Bill In terms of pure mathematics, you've written two of the books?

Nutley Yes.

Bill So what do you need me for? You've written two books all on your own. Seems to me you're doing very canny under your own steam.

Nutley I'd like you to read the first two books and advise me about the third.

Bill Fair enough. Drop in next time you're passing and leave what you've done so far. I'll give it the old once-over and——

Nutley (*breaking in*) I've brought the manuscripts with me.

Bill You have?

Nutley Yes.

Bill Whereabouts?

Nutley They're in the box. (*He draws Bill's attention to the large cardboard box*)

Bill I thought I heard a rustling.

Ellen is intrigued by the remark, but says nothing. Nutley ignores it, and removes the lid of the box. From it he brings two huge typewritten manuscripts: around five hundred pages each. He places them on the bench near Bill

Nutley Volume One. Volume Two.

Bill And ... one to come.

Nutley One to come.

Bill Well that's ... grand.

Ellen *For Whom the Bell Tolls.*

They look across at her. She holds up a book

Hemingway.

Bill Good. (*His attention returns to the Nutley manuscripts. They are huge and forbidding*)

Nutley You'll be very careful with them, won't you?

Bill Oh yes, I'll be careful. I mean, the way I look at it, civilization moves forward about one inch every century, and this might be the book to do it.

Nutley Thank you.

Bill And bearing in mind it's a trilogy, well, that's three inches, isn't it?

A glare from Ellen. Bill smiles back

Ellen I wonder ... may I join in?

Bill Join in what? We're only talking.

Ellen It's such a small room and I couldn't help overhearing your stimulating discussion. I realize I'm only a Council employee *and* a woman but——

Bill I'm sure we welcome all constructive remarks, don't we, Mr Nutley?

Nutley By all means.

Ellen It's just a simple question that I was hoping Mr Robson would ask you, but he seems to have overlooked it in his excitement.

Bill Carry on. We enjoy simple questions.

Ellen What is your trilogy about?

Bill Oh, yes, that *is* a good question. (*And maybe it's his turn to give Ellen a glare*)

Ellen I thought so.

Bill Mind you, will it spoil the enjoyment of reading the manuscripts if I already know what I'm going to read about? What do you think? (*He puts the questions to Nutley*)

Nutley I don't think it'll spoil anything. The trilogy is about Lorca.

Ellen Lorca. Really. Fascinating. (*Satisfied she's dropped Bill in it, she returns to her keyboard*)

Bill So it's about Lorca is it?

Nutley Yes. Are you interested in Lorca?

Bill Oh yes. Fascinated. (*He flips through the first two or three pages of the manuscript, squinting for clues. He finds just enough to help him out*) Ah now, I see it's *Federico* Lorca you're about . . .

Nutley Of course. Who else?

Bill Well, see, I'm just a proletarian pitman, but there's a canny lad called Lorca plays midfield for Athletico Madrid. But I don't suppose anybody'd be likely to write a book about him. Definitely not three books. He's a good player, mind . . . quick on the turn . . .

Nutley This is Lorca the playwright.

Bill Why of course, I realize that now. (*Another flip through the pages, playing for time*) And a good playwright, an' all.

Nutley A great playwright.

Bill Certainly. The question is . . . did he achieve it or was it thrust upon him? I'll tell you what. I'll read all this and see if it tells me the answer. (*He stands up*) So I think your best plan's to leave me to get on with it. Unless there's anything else you want to ask me. Like, in the skill and expertise department . . .

Nutley How long will it take you to read?

Bill Difficult to say. I've been a bit swamped with aspiring writers already, so let's see . . .

Ellen Why don't you leave your address and telephone number, Mr Nutley? Then Mr Robson can contact you as soon as he's read your work and done his critical analysis.

Bill Yes, good idea, it's what we've done with the others, isn't it?

Nutley My address and phone number are on the manuscripts.

Bill It's been a pleasure to do business with you, Mr Nutley.

Nutley Thank you, Mr Robson. (*He turns to Ellen*) I hope I didn't disturb you too much.

Ellen I don't disturb easily.

Nutley Fine.

He hesitates, then goes

Bill watches him off the premises

Bill That went well, didn't it?
Ellen I suppose it could have been more embarrassing. Just.
Bill Oh howay, I did all right.
Ellen For an amateur. It was rather like watching an amateur dentist.
Bill No idea, never watched one. But then, you're more sophisticated than I am. (*He picks up the manuscripts and tries them for weight*) Ye bugger. It weighs a ton. I never thought writing would be this heavy.
Ellen Exceedingly long words, probably.
Bill And had you really heard of this lad Lorca? That wasn't just for show, like?
Ellen Of course I've heard of him. I've even read his work. Federico García Lorca, Spanish poet and dramatist.
Bill When he first said it, I thought he meant Lorca the killer whale.
Ellen Yes, you would.
Bill Or else Lorca the Greek.
Ellen Zorba the Greek.
Bill I knew I was probably wrong. That's why I didn't say anything. About Greeks or killer whales. (*He resumes his place, manuscripts on his knee*)

Ellen sits down at her keyboard

Is he still in work, then, old Lorca?
Ellen No. He was murdered during the Spanish Civil War.
Bill Getaway. Who killed him?
Ellen The fascists.
Bill General Franco's mob?

Reaction from Ellen. Bill smiles

That surprised you. I know about the Spanish Civil War. Part of my proletarian heritage.
Ellen Good.
Bill Why did they kill him? Did they not like his poems and plays?
Ellen Not funny, Mr Robson.
Bill Don't suppose it was a whole heap of laughs for old Lorca, either.
Ellen I have a suggestion to make.
Bill I should write a poem and get myself shot?
Ellen Read your book.
Bill I enjoy talking, you're very interesting to talk to——
Ellen (*breaking in as she sees/hears a customer come into the library*) I have a customer.
Bill If it's another trilogy, tell them I've got a headache.

Ellen exits, then returns almost immediately with Nutley

Nutley Sorry, it's me again.
Bill You haven't written Volume Three already?
Nutley No. It isn't that. I would like to borrow a book.
Bill Well you couldn't have come to a better place. We've got thousands of books. Mrs Scott knows where they all are.
Nutley *Your* book, Mr Robson.

Bill My book?

Nutley Your slim volume of poems.

Bill Certainly. (*He looks around the room, finds the exercise book. He hands it to Nutley*)

Nutley I'd just be very interested to read some of your work.

Bill And you might pick up some useful hints. You'll find there's some good stuff in there.

Nutley Thank you.

Bill Now, if you'll excuse me, I've got a canny bit homework to get on with.

Nutley Of course. I hope you enjoy it. (*He looks from one to the other*) Good-morning.

Nutley exits

Ellen Forgive my saying so, but aren't you ever so slightly out of your mind?

Bill Why?

Ellen I think there's every chance Mr Nutley will recognize the poems in your book and realize you stole them.

Bill That's all right. I'll tell him I gave him the wrong book. I'll say that's the one I use for practising.

Ellen And if he asks to read the proper book . . . the one with your own original work in it? What then?

Bill Well he can't. I haven't written any original work so obviously he can't look at it.

Ellen Will you tell him that?

Bill Certainly not. I'll tell him something else.

Ellen You'll tell him a lie?

Bill Probably. What else is there? Don't worry. Nobody's going to get hurt.

She sighs, giving up on logical debate, and resumes work at her keyboard. Bill starts reading Nutley's manuscript. She clicks. He reads. Then:

What does "plangent" mean? (*He pronounces it with a hard "g"*)

Ellen Plangent. (*She pronounces it correctly*)

So does Bill, the second time

Bill Plangent then. What does it mean?

Ellen Insistent and vibrating. In some ways, you are plangent Mr Robson. Very plangent.

Bill Thank you. (*He translates it into a compliment*)

He continues to read. She continues to click

I'm sorry to be plangent again but can I ask you something else?

Ellen So far, I haven't discovered the secret of stopping you.

Bill Do you read a lot of books?

Ellen Yes. Quite a lot.

Bill I just ask because people that work in chocolate factories get that they can't stand the sight of chocolates.

Ellen And you thought because I spend my life dealing with books, I might get tired of reading them. The answer is no, I don't get tired of reading books.

Bill How many do you read? One a week? One a fortnight?

Ellen I don't keep count. Probably three or four in a week.

Bill Ye bugger. That's amazing. That's ... two hundred a year.

Ellen I'm not trying to break records. I just like reading books.

Bill (*after hesitating*) Would you like to read this one?

Ellen (*wary*) Er ... which one?

Bill Two-thirds of Mr Nutley's trilogy?

Ellen Just a moment ...

Bill I'm sure you'll enjoy it, it's all about Lorca you know ...

Ellen May I translate this conversation into plain English?

Bill If you think it'll help.

Ellen You want me to read the manuscript. What will you do while I read the manuscript?

Bill I will *not* read the manuscript. Obviously. 'Cos you'll be reading it.

Ellen So, having got the job under false pretences, you're now proposing that I do the job for you?

Bill I admit it seems like that. But the way I look at it is this. You know about books. You know what to look for. It's like me going to a football match. I know what to look for. I don't with books. So what I thought was ... you read the book ... tell me what you think about it ... and I'll pass the message on to Mr Nutley when he comes back. He's going to be better off with your opinions than mine. I'm just thinking about the customer.

Ellen And you'll be able to sit around all day, while I do my job and yours.

Bill Oh no. I'll do your job.

Ellen What?

Bill I'll do your job. (*He gets up and crosses to the keyboard*) I can do that.

Ellen You can't. I went on a special course.

Bill How long for?

Ellen (*after a slight hesitation*) Half a day.

Bill Listen. All you're doing is putting the books on to computer. Title. Author's name. Reference number. I know all about that stuff. I used to play space invaders every night at the miners' welfare. There's nothing I don't know about computers.

Ellen I don't see what space invaders have to do with it.

Bill I have invaded your space. I'm trying to make it easier for both of us. (*He returns to his place, collects the manuscript and takes it to her. He presents it, with some reverence*) Federico García Lorca. The inside story.

Against this we gently fade in a fragment of the Miles Davis/Gil Evans "Sketches of Spain". This carries us over a time gap of a week or so. The Lights fade to black, then up again, fairly swiftly to ...

SCENE 3

Ellen sits in Bill's place, reading the manuscript. She is not enjoying it

Bill walks in from the lending library. He's very chirpy

Bill Hey, it's great being a librarian, isn't it? I've just done two Barbara Cartlands, a Catherine Cookson and a Louis Alcott. (*He pronounces it "Lewis"*)
Ellen Louisa.
Bill What?
Ellen Louisa Alcott. Louisa May Alcott.
Bill Never mind. Whatever his real name, I sent my customers away with the books they wanted and smiles on their faces with my cheerful Geordie humour. But this is the bit I really enjoy. (*He sits down at the keyboard and starts clicking away with great gusto and enthusiasm. He talks to himself as he types in the details of the next book. His manner is that of a bingo caller*) And it's eyes down for your next star attraction ... *Literature and Western Man* by J. B. Priestley, published by your friend and mine, canny Will Heinemann, in the year of Our Lord nineteen hundred and sixty and still right up there in the charts——
Ellen (*interrupting him*) Forgive my being plangent, but may I ask a question?
Bill Certainly you can, I'm here to help.
Ellen Have you considered working quietly?
Bill I've never been able to work quietly.
Ellen You must have been very popular at the coal face.
Bill I was. Used to sing all day.
Ellen Sing? Oh God.
Bill Never stopped.
Ellen Traditional folk songs about the misery of the miners' lot?
Bill That's right. Like *Blue Suede Shoes* and *I Wanna be Bobby's Girl*. I used to tell a lot of jokes as well. They were very popular.
Ellen I bet they were.
Bill Would you like to hear a joke?
Ellen No thank you.
Bill I know hundreds.
Ellen When I feel myself in urgent need of a joke, I'll let you know.
Bill Right.
Ellen Now let's see if we can both work quietly.
Bill OK.

They work quietly for a while, then:

Ellen Something else I wanted to ask you ...
Bill Shhh! I'm trying to work quietly.
Ellen I thought I heard a rustling.
Bill Did you? (*He looks around for clues*)
Ellen I don't mean now. I mean, you said it to Mr Nutley last week and I

didn't understand what you were talking about. And I like to understand. Everything, if possible.

Bill Have you heard of Jimmy James?

Ellen Jesse's lesser-known brother?

Bill No. He was a great comedian. From Stockton-on-Tees. Where's that box? (*He looks around for Nutley's box*)

Ellen finds it and hands it to him

Ellen This one?

Bill (*taking the box*) I need you to help me. Stand up and hold that.

Ellen takes the box, as instructed. She stands beside Bill

Ellen Like this?

Bill Perfect. Now, I'm Jimmy James, right? I'm smoking a cigarette and I'm a bit drunk. (*Which he mimes*) And you've just come back from two years as Colonial Secretary in Egypt.

Ellen I don't remember.

Bill For the purposes of the sketch.

Ellen I see.

Bill Now. I say to you ... "Did they give you a present?" (*Then he says it, as Jimmy James*) Did they give you a present?

Ellen What do I say?

Bill You say ... "Yes, I was presented with a pair of man-eating lions."

Ellen In Egypt?

Bill For the purposes of the (sketch).

Ellen (*chiming in*) The purposes of the sketch. Right. (*And she plays the line*) Yes, they presented me with a pair of man-eating lions.

Bill Where do you keep them?

Ellen I've no idea.

Bill points at the box. Ellen gets the idea

Ellen Sorry. Got it. Understood. Let's do it all again from the beginning.

Bill Righto.

Ellen Hey, this is fun, isn't it? Much better than being a librarian or a writer-in-residence. (*Then she slips into the part*) I've just come back from two years as Colonial Secretary in Egypt.

Bill Did they give you a present?

Ellen Yes. I was presented with a pair of man-eating lions.

Bill Where do you keep them?

Ellen In the box.

Bill reacts, in character, then:

Bill I thought I heard a rustling.

Ellen mouths the words along with him, then laughs

Ellen Yes, that's rather good. What else happens?

Bill Well, it turns out there's a giraffe in the box and an elephant, and at the end he says: "There'll be room in the van for the three of us."

Ellen The three of us?

Bill I haven't bothered telling you about Eli.

Ellen No, don't bother telling me about Eli. (*She sits down*) I really enjoyed that.

Bill Good.

Ellen Do you know any more?

Bill Yes, lots. But I've got to get to my work. (*He goes back to the keyboard*)

Ellen You were right of course.

Bill I'm always right. But I don't know what you're talking about.

Ellen Mr Nutley came in to see you about his trilogy. You said to him: "Where is the manuscript?" He said to you: "In the box." You said to him: "I thought I heard a rustling."

Bill I still don't understand, pet, I mean, Mrs Scott.

Ellen I have now finished reading the first two volumes of Mr Nutley's trilogy.

Bill That's grand.

Ellen shakes her head

   Not grand?

Ellen It has been the worst experience of my life.

Bill It depends what other experiences you've had.

Ellen The other bad experiences are not your business. This one *is* your business. You will have to tell Mr Nutley that his book is pretentious and boring. The grammar and syntax are disgraceful. The style is non-existent. The spelling is deplorable. And it's badly typed.

Bill Did you enjoy the story?

Ellen I'm still looking for the story.

Bill I'm glad I didn't bother reading it.

Ellen But you'll have to tell him.

Bill That's all right.

Ellen Or you could read it yourself. You might disagree.

Bill No, I'll take your word. I'll give him a ring tomorrow. See when he's free for a bollocking. (*He sees somebody in the library*) Excuse me. Customer. Unless you want to go?

Ellen Carry on.

Bill I don't want it to turn into a demarcation issue, like.

Ellen I'm sure it's a ratepayer desperate for some cheerful Geordie humour.

Bill I expect so.

Bill exits

Ellen starts to make notes on a pad about the Nutley manuscript. Before she can get very far . . .

Bill returns with Bernard, an amiable youth of twenty or so, carrying the tools of the surveying trade—clipboard, pencils and one, or maybe two, measuring tapes. Bernard may well be street-wise but the evidence is he is not library-back-room-wise. He stares about him

   It wasn't a customer. It was Bernard.

Ellen Good-morning, Bernard.
Bernard Hi.
Ellen What have you written, Bernard? Please God, not a trilogy.
Bernard What?
Bill Bernard's from the surveyor's department.
Ellen That doesn't rule out creative writing. Thomas Hardy was an architect.
Bill He's here to do some surveying.
Ellen (*shrugging*) What else can a surveyor do?
Bernard Got to measure up the rooms.
Ellen Fine.
Bernard Right.
Ellen I have to make some notes on two-thirds of a trilogy. Mr Robson's busy storing information. You have to measure up the room. We should be able to co-exist, don't you think?
Bernard What?
Bill Just carry on, son. It'll soon be time for the next tea-break. Life's like that in the middle classes.

They drift into their respective activities. Ellen makes notes. Bill feeds information. Bernard takes measurements in an aimless and uncertain way. Out of the more-or-less silence:

Did you say you were making notes on Mr Nutley's trilogy?
Bernard What?
Ellen Yes. So you'll know what to tell him.
Bill Will I understand them?
Ellen I'll keep them *very* simple.
Bill Ta.

Bill is about to re-start work at his keyboard, only to discover he is in Bernard's way. It is impossible to carry out a survey in a working environment without being a damned nuisance. In this case, Bernard needs to measure a ceiling height or a window opening — something of the sort. Naturally curious, Bill watches him

Is this a proper job you've got, son, or are you on a scheme?
Bernard Yes. (*Partly because he's concentrating on his work, partly because he doesn't grasp the question*)
Bill That's nice.
Bernard I mean, like basically, I just get sent out to measure things up.
Bill It's a dangerous world we live in, Bernard. But with you to help, at least we'll know how big it is.
Ellen It's no good, I can't go on. (*She sets aside her notebook and pen*)
Bill Oh howay, pet, you've got the best years of your life ahead of you yet.
Ellen Life's all right. It's Mr Nutley's so-called book I can't cope with.
Bill There's no problem. Forget about it. (*He crosses to look at what she's written in her notebook. Reading her notes*) Is this what you really think?
Ellen (*flatly*) Yes.

Bill indicates a word she's written

Bill That's not a very nice word to use.
Ellen It's true.
Bill And you an educated woman ...
Ellen If you'd had to read all that stuff ... (*she points at the piled-up manuscripts*) ... you'd certainly use language of that kind.
Bill I see.
Ellen Mr Nutley should be banned for life from using sharp instruments like pens and pencils. Also, possibly from food, water and oxygen.

The telephone rings and she crosses to answer it

(*On the phone*) Eastwood Road branch library. ... Hallo, Mr Nutley, we were just talking about you. ... Just one moment, here is our writer-in-residence to speak to you ... (*She hands the receiver to Bill. Her expression says: the buck stops here*)

Bernard manages to get in the way of both of them in a gentle and harmless way. Eventually, Bill speaks to Nutley

Bill Good-morning, Mr Nutley, how are you keeping? ... And the creative juices, still hot and strong, are they? ... That's grand. ... What? ... Oh, yes, we've read the book. ... No, I mean *I've* read the book, well, obviously, I'm the writer-in-residence, that's my job, reading books. ... Skill and expertise, exactly. ... What? Well, I don't think it's fair to do these things over the phone, do you? ... Any time at all, to suit you, the customer's always right, what? ... Ay, this afternoon's fine, we should have the surveyors out by then. ... No, it's only Bernard, he's a canny lad. ... Right then ... mind how you go ... tata ... (*He hangs up*)
Ellen Since we were in the same room, I couldn't help overhearing. Mr Nutley's coming in here this afternoon?
Bill He's in the area today.
Ellen He's in the area every day. He *lives* in the area. Sorry, Bernard ... (*As once more she's in his way*)

She and Bill have to cross to another part of the room to continue their discussion

So what will you tell him?
Bill I'll tell him, as a writer, he's useless.
Ellen Just like that?
Bill You tell me he's useless. You know what you're talking about. You read two hundred books a year. I'll pass the message on. Mr Nutley, you're useless, I'll say.
Ellen He won't like it.
Bill Hard luck. If it comes to a fight, I'm bigger than him.
Ellen No fights please. There's an obscure Council by-law that prohibits bare-knuckle fights on library premises.
Bill I'll reason with him. I'll say look, what's the point of cluttering up the place with useless books when there isn't enough room for the books

we've got? I'll tell him how you've been complaining for years about the lack of space here and how you've been pestering the libraries committee to build you an extension and——

Ellen I've been pestering the libraries committee to build me an extension . . .
Bill I just said that. You told me about it yesterday. And the day before.
Ellen Bernard . . .
Bill What? Oh. You mean . . .

They both turn to look at Bernard who continues with his painstaking measuring and recording

Bernard . . .
Bernard What?
Ellen I thought I heard a rustling.
Bernard A rustling? (*He listens. He can't hear anything*)
Ellen Is that why you're here?
Bernard I'm here to measure up the room.
Ellen Is that all?
Bernard No.
Ellen There's something else?
Bernard Yes. I have to measure up the other rooms as well.
Ellen But why?
Bernard Why what?
Bill *Why* are you measuring up the rooms?
Bernard To see how big they are.
Bill Information technology. It's everywhere you look.
Ellen Now Bernard, please don't think I'm prying, but I like to know everything. You are collecting and collating information.
Bernard I'm measuring up the library.
Ellen And when you've finished, what will you do?

Bernard has to take a run at this thought

Bernard I'll . . . go back to the office.
Ellen And then what happens?
Bernard Depends what time it is. I'll probably miss the tea break.
Bill I'll put the kettle on. (*Bill organizes the kettle during the following sequence*)
Ellen What will happen to your measurements?
Bernard Like these? (*He shows her the work he's done on his clipboard*)
Ellen Yes. Like these.
Bernard I'll put them on a proper big drawing.
Ellen I see. (*She begins to feel she's getting somewhere*) So now we have a proper big drawing of the library . . .
Bernard Not now. It'll take me ages.
Bill Listen, son, I'll tell you what Mrs Scott wants to know. She wants to know if you doing the survey means the Council's going to build her an extension. 'Cos she needs an extension, see? On account of there isn't enough room to store all the books. And that's a big problem if you're a library.

Bernard Yes.

It's unclear what he means. They seek clarification

Bill Does that mean, yes, there's going to be an extension?
Bernard No. It means yes, storage is a big problem.

Ellen's patience begins to run out

Ellen Oh, for God's sake, do you have any idea at all what you're doing here?
Bernard Yes, I'm measuring up the rooms.
Ellen We've just about got that clear in our heads. The point is, do you have any idea what the Council's plans are for the library?
Bernard Oh no, that's impossible.
Ellen I was always taught nothing's impossible.
Bernard I think it's impossible to know about the Council's plans because mostly the Council doesn't know itself what their plans are, mostly.
Ellen But has there been talk in your office about building an extension to the library. You know, over your tea breaks?
Bernard Oh yes, there's always talk. Lots of talk. Extensions, stuff like that. But I'm not allowed to discuss anything. They tell us that. Don't say nothing, or else the ratepayers might find out.
Bill Seems to me there might be an extension or, on the other hand, there might not.
Bernard Yes. That's it.
Ellen It all sounds like the clear-sighted, go-ahead policy of a hung council.
Bernard You should hear what Mr Carruthers has to say.

Bernard is beginning to get the hang of conversation as an enjoyable filler of time. Bill and Ellen both respond to the name Carruthers — mainly because it's a new element in the discussion

Ellen Mr Carruthers?
Bernard You should hear what he says.
Bill Who's Mr Carruthers?
Bernard I work for him.
Ellen He's the Borough Surveyor.
Bernard (*shrugging*) Don't know what he does. I just work for him.
Ellen And what does he say that we should hear?

Bernard has forgotten where he came into this section of the debate

Bernard What?
Bill You said we should hear what Mr Carruthers has to say.
Ellen I think it was on the subject of the hung Council.
Bernard Oh yes. He says hanging's too good for them. He says they should be drawn and quartered. As well.

Bill sees somebody come into the library

Bill There's a coincidence.
Ellen What is?

Bill Mr Carruthers thinks the Council should be hung, drawn and quartered and here comes a real-live councillor . . .

As Councillor Graham enters, in time to hear the gist of Bill's statement

Graham Did I overhear you discussing the Council?
Bill Humble voters taking a keen interest in local democracy.
Ellen Good-morning, Councillor Graham.
Graham Good-morning, Mrs Scott. (*Graham is nervously cheerful. She turns to Bernard with a polite, who-the-hell-is-this? look on her face*) And this is . . . ?
Bill Bernard.
Ellen From the surveyor's office.
Bill Mr Carruthers sent him to measure us up.
Graham Oh yes. Of course. I understand.
Ellen You do?
Bill As a matter of fact, we're all getting a bit excited.
Graham Really?
Bill Yes. Because I happen to know Mrs Scott's been on at your committee for years about an extension to the library. Too many books, you see, and not enough space.
Graham We do appreciate your problems, Mrs Scott . . .
Ellen Thank you. (*Ellen accepts it as a politico's bromide. She's a good judge*)
Bill And where I come from, if the surveyors move in, it generally means the builders are not far behind. That's why we're getting excited.
Graham I see. (*She turns to Bernard*) Er . . . Bernard. It is all right if I call you Bernard?
Bernard I don't mind. Being as how it's my name.
Graham I need to talk to Mrs Scott in private.
Bernard Yes. (*He doesn't understand what it's got to do with him*)
Graham What we have to discuss is confidential.
Bernard That's OK. It's none of my business anyway. (*He makes no move to leave*)
Ellen (*intervening*) Bernard, I think what Councillor Graham means is, could you measure something else for a while? Like the front door? Or perhaps the drains?
Bernard I don't do drains.
Ellen Doors?
Bernard Oh yes, I do doors.
Bill Hadaway and do a few doors. There's a good lad.
Bernard I get it. You want me out of the way?
Ellen Yes please, but nicely.
Bernard That's OK. I'm dead good at doors. Doors . . .

Bernard exits, in pursuit of doors

Bill (*calling after him*) You'll find one near where you came in . . . (*Then Bill turns to Graham*) Is it all right if I stay? Or is it confidential from me as well?

Graham You work here, therefore it concerns you, Mr Robson. Though it concerns Mrs Scott rather more.

Bill I'll try not to talk too much.

Ellen May we have that in writing?

Bill You know me. I'm not very good at writing.

They realize their private world is tending to exclude Graham

Ellen Sorry. We tend to get carried away with our friendly badinage about the workplace.

Bill That's true. Fire away, Councillor. Tell us about the new extension.

Graham It isn't quite as simple as that.

Bill You're going to build an *old* extension?

Graham (*after hesitating*) There is a meeting of the Libraries Sub-Committee this evening. We shall be asked to approve a rationalization programme for the libraries service.

Bill What does that mean in English?

Graham Essentially we are taking on board the task of providing a library and information service to the ratepayers, geared to the needs of the twenty-first century.

Bill But what does it mean in English?

Ellen (*to Bill*) You said you wouldn't talk too much. (*Ellen is irritated by Bill's aggression towards Graham*)

Bill Where I come from, whenever anybody talks about rationalization, it means they're going to close things. Nobody ever closed my pit. It was just rationalized out of existence. Over a weekend. (*He turns to Graham*) Is that the coded message? Are you going to close this place?

Pause. Graham says nothing. Ellen realizes the truth of the situation

Ellen Is it true?

Bill Of course it's true. I know a rustling when I hear one.

Graham It isn't quite as simple as that.

Ellen It never is.

Graham As you know, this library is close to the supermarket. The supermarket chain would like to buy the property. In fact, they've made a very generous offer.

Ellen And the Council has accepted the offer?

Graham No. It isn't quite . . . (as simple as that).

Bill (*finishing it for her*) Quite as simple as that.

Graham The Tories on the committee want to accept the offer. Naturally enough. The Socialists want to turn it down. Naturally enough.

Ellen And the Liberal-Democrats?

Graham It seems to us there are sound and persuasive arguments on both sides . . .

Bill Naturally enough.

Graham But we are likely to recommend selling this branch to the supermarket.

Ellen I see. (*She crosses to the window. She looks out*) If I look out of this window, I can count . . . one, two, three, four, five, six, seven, eight, nine places where I can buy a packet of tea, a bag of sugar, five pounds of potatoes or the metric equivalent. And I'm not even wearing my distance glasses. It seems to me, Councillor, that whatever your community is lacking, it is not retail grocery outlets. On the other hand, knowing how much you like to hear what lies on the other hand ... (*again she looks out*) ... there isn't a lending library in sight. (*She turns to Graham*) Does anything strike you about what I can see out of my window?

Graham Believe me, I do understand. You've spent many years in this branch and the committee does appreciate, as I do, the dedication and devotion——

Bill (*breaking in*) Councillor!

Graham Yes, Mr Robson?

Bill Hadaway to hell.

Graham I'm sorry?

Bill It's a well-known phrase or saying, where I come from. A homely piece of proletarian vernacular. It means I would rather, for the moment, you and me were in different rooms ... or different streets ... or different towns ... like ... hadaway to hell.

Graham Thank you, Mr Robson. Your meaning is quite clear. And again, believe me, I do understand ...

Bill You don't understand anything! I mean, for a start, I bet you haven't got the faintest idea how civilization makes progress. Now, I'll admit it's only about one inch every hundred years but——

Ellen (*breaking in*) Leave it, Bill. It doesn't matter.

Bill It *does* matter.

Ellen It's my library. My dedication. My devotion. Leave it.

Pause. Bill turns to Graham

Bill Are you still here, Councillor?

Graham (*looking at her watch*) Now you mention it, I do have a Social Services Advisory committee in half-an-hour's time ...

Bill Better not keep them waiting, Councillor. They might be stuck for a balanced argument.

Graham I am sorry, Mrs Scott.

She considers saying something to Bill, but changes her mind and exits

Ellen sits down, trying to absorb the news. Out of a thoughtful silence:

Ellen I thought I heard a rustling.

Bill Politicians rustle all the time.

Ellen But thank you for fighting my battle.

Bill And thank you.

Ellen What for?

Bill Didn't you notice? You called me Bill.

Ellen Well. There aren't many of us left.

Bernard returns

Bernard Can I come back in?

Bill Have you finished measuring the front door?
Bernard No, but it's coming on to rain. (*He resumes measuring the room*)

Ellen registers what he's doing

Ellen We thought instant coffee over here ... frozen foods over there ...
toilet rolls on this wall ...
Bernard Sorry. Don't know what you're talking about.
Ellen Civilization.
Bernard Oh. That. (*He shrugs and carries on*)

The Lights slowly fade to—

BLACK-OUT

ACT II

The library, a couple of hours later

A little blues over: Miles Davis playing "Star People"

Bill and Ellen are sitting in their respective places, doing nothing perceptible. The overall impression is they're waiting for Godot, with neither hope nor expectation—which is, of course, about right for Godot

The music fades. They sit. A long, long silence then:

Bill It's going well, isn't it?
Ellen Is it?
Bill Oh yes.
Ellen I wouldn't know. I've never been on strike before.
Bill Definitely beginning to bite.

Another long silence as they continue with their strike action

Ellen Whom?
Bill Eh?
Ellen Whom are we beginning to bite?
Bill The other side. Management.
Ellen We haven't told management we're on strike. In fact, it's fair to say that nobody in the entire world knows that we're on strike. I'm no expert, but that must limit its effect.
Bill Wait till we start turning customers away.
Ellen To do that, we need customers.

Bill lifts his hand indicating: listen. There is the sound of the outside library door and footsteps from the lending library. They both get up

Bill Leave this to me, comrade. I've been on more picket lines than you've read trilogies.

Ellen shrugs and gives way

   Bill exits

Ellen picks up the telephone and dials a number. She listens. She doesn't hear anything helpful. She hangs up

   Bill returns

We are on our way.

Ellen You just bit somebody?

Bill Better than that. I just bit an old-age pensioner.

Ellen A mortal wound?

Bill Mrs Dickenson. Popped in for her Barbara Cartland.

Ellen She generally does that on a Tuesday.

Bill I said: "Sorry Mrs D. There is no way Barbara Cartland is prepared to cross a picket line."

Ellen If Barbara Cartland saw a picket line, she'd probably want to shoot it.

Bill There wasn't time to consult her.

Ellen And Mrs Dickenson ... did she reel back as if bitten?

Bill Hard to say. Poor old soul, she's a bit deaf. (*He sits down. Adopts his strike posture*)

Bill They shall not pass.

Ellen Mr Robson, with the greatest of respect ...

Bill When people say with the greatest of respect, it generally means they haven't got any. Respect.

Ellen This is a load of bollocks.

Bill You reckon?

Ellen If we're on strike, we should let people know. We should have placards and banners and a brazier. Like you see on Channel Four news.

Bill You can't do any of that till you've had a secret ballot.

Ellen I took the first step.

Bill What have you been doing? Learning to make the sign of a cross?

Ellen I telephoned the union office.

Bill When?

Ellen While you were biting old Mrs Dickenson.

Bill What did the union have to say?

Ellen I got a recorded message saying the office is closed for the Easter holiday.

Bill Easter was weeks ago.

Ellen So?

Bill ponders this

Bill So, you're dealing with a union that's inefficient and out of touch with the rank and file. Therefore we have to continue with our unofficial action.

Ellen Old-age pensioners dropping dead through lack of intellectual nourishment?

Bill Definitely.

Ellen I still don't see how depriving old people of Barbara Cartland will bring management to its knees.

Bill We'll think of some other things to do as well. You see, what happened, when I was down the pit ... there'd be a dispute ... maybes about overtime or bonuses or safety ... first thing you do, you walk out. Walk out, take a deep breath, work out your strategy. We're still in the first stage.

Ellen We haven't actually walked out.

Bill Well, no, but it's warmer in here, isn't it?

Ellen All right. We've walked out, while remaining seated more or less throughout. Shall we work out our strategy?

Bill Fine by me, pet.

Ellen Hamster.

Bill Sorry, comrade.

Ellen Strategy.

They think about strategy. Nothing much happens

Well?

Bill Have you got any ideas?

Ellen You're the expert on industrial relations.

Bill Labour relations. Management and the media call it industrial relations. We of the proletariat call it labour relations.

Ellen And having decided what to call it, how do you do it?

Bill Let's think. What is it we're trying to do?

Ellen Keep this place open.

Bill Exactly.

Ellen And the decision to close it is likely to be taken at a meeting this evening.

Bill Well, I'll tell you something for nothing.

Ellen What?

Bill We've got to move fast.

Ellen And as Edith Cavell somehow forgot to say, old Mrs Dickenson is not enough.

Bill What?

Ellen sees a customer come in

Ellen Customer. Is it my turn to be the picket line?

Bill Yes. Can you manage?

Ellen As long as it's someone really old and really deaf.

Ellen exits

Bill sings quietly to himself: "Here we go, here we go, here we go ..."

Ellen returns with Nutley

Ellen Somebody to see you.

Bill Sorry, I'm on strike. I can't see anybody. (*Then he sees who it is*)

Nutley It's me.

Bill So I see.

Nutley We have an appointment. You telephoned this morning.

Bill Ah, well, see, a lot of things have happened since this morning, bonny lad. We've had the surveyors in, and a visit from Councillor Graham, Deputy-Co-Chair-Person of the Libraries Sub-Committee to tell us we're going to be a supermarket extension.

Nutley I only understood a little bit of that.

Ellen The Council is going to close this library.

Nutley But they can't! (*He's genuinely outraged*)

Ellen They seem to be under the impression that they can.

Bill It's called democracy. Doing dirty things on people from a great height.

Ellen So Mr Robson suggested strike action.

Bill Technically speaking, you just crossed a picket line.

Nutley I didn't see a picket line.

Ellen We've sent away for some donkey jackets and a riot squad but they quoted ten days for delivery.

Bill Also, we're having the picket line indoors, because it's warmer.

Nutley That was your advice, as a veteran of the miners' strike? Industrial action?

Bill Definitely. You're speaking to a fully paid-up enemy within.

Nutley I see. (*He ponders the implications of all this then:*) Have you been turning people away?

Ellen Oh yes. The old-age pensioners have been getting very short shrift, I can promise you.

Bill Especially if they're deaf.

Nutley How does this apply to writers?

Bill Sorry. Don't understand, kiddar.

Nutley I'm no ordinary citizen here for my weekly fix of Archer or Forsyth. I am a writer.

Bill Nobody's disputing that. Not yet anyway.

Nutley Without writers there would be no libraries.

Ellen Without readers there wouldn't be an awful lot.

Nutley I'm here as a writer, to discuss my work with you, Mr Robson, and to avail myself of your skill and expertise.

Bill But can't you see? If I talk to you about your work, that makes me a scab. A blackleg. And scum. All three.

Nutley Can't we rise above all that?

Ellen No, I don't think you can rise above it. You could try shifting to one side.

Bill What does that mean?

Ellen Obviously you and Mr Nutley could spend hours talking to each other about whether you should talk to each other. I'd like to suggest you simply talk to each other.

Bill Sorry. I don't think we should talk to each other. What do you think? (*He addresses the question to Nutley*)

Nutley I think we should talk to each other.

Ellen We could have a secret ballot.

Bill A secret ballot?

Ellen Why not?

Bill How would you organize it?

Ellen Get a piece of paper. Tear it into three. Take one each. Vote Yes or No. Count the votes. Act according to the will of the majority.

Bill I can't see it ever working in practice, but I'm game if you are.

Ellen Are you game, Mr Nutley?

Nutley Yes.

Bill Does he get a vote?

Nutley I don't see why not. This is universal adult franchise, save only it's restricted to the three of us. It's a ballot of free-thinking individuals, making their decisions as mature, educated citizens in a civilized and cultured society.

Pause

Bill Righto. Carry on.

Ellen takes a sheet of paper and tears it into three. She gives one each to Bill and Nutley and keeps one for herself

Ellen Vote. Yes if you're in favour of Mr Robson keeping his appointment with Mr Nutley, and No if you're against.
Bill Got it.

They write their votes on their pieces of paper

Ellen Now. We need a ballot box.
Bill I always travel with a ballot box. (*He takes his cap from its hook and hands it to her*)

Ellen collects the votes in the cap

Ellen We also need a returning officer.
Bill I'm happy for you to be the returning officer. Unless you'd rather elect one by secret ballot. (*He turns to Nutley, inviting his opinion*)
Nutley (*to Ellen*) I'm sure we're all happy for you to be the returning officer.
Ellen Thank you. (*She empties the votes on to her desk and counts them. Then she turns to the electorate*) I, being the official returning officer, duly declare that the votes cast were as follows. Two votes Yes. One vote No.
Bill Two-one. What was the half-time score?
Ellen Why don't you talk to Mr Nutley about his trilogy?
Bill I'd just like to thank my opponent for a good clean fight and——
Ellen (*breaking in*) Mr Robson!
Bill Yes?

Ellen finds the box containing the Nutley manuscripts and thrusts it at Bill

Ellen Manuscript. Trilogy. Lorca. Author. Writer-in-residence. Skill and expertise. Talk.
Bill Got the message. Loud and clear. (*He turns to Nutley*) Brace yourself, son, because this is going to hurt you more than it hurts me.

Nutley braces himself—though at this stage he assumes Bill is joking. Bill opens the box and brings out the notes written by Ellen

Ready?
Nutley Ready.
Bill Now we've read your books——
Nutley We?
Bill We meaning I. I've read your books. The first two volumes of your trilogy. And this is what I think. (*A beat then:*) You don't mind constructive criticism?
Nutley That's why I'm here, Mr Robson.
Bill Good. Grand. Well, for a kick-off, generally speaking, it's been the

worst experience of my life. And believe me, I've had some bad ones, bearing in mind all those years down the pit. I found your work pretentious and boring. Your grammar and syntax are disgraceful. Your style is non-existent. Your spelling is deplorable. And you can't type. My recommendation is that you be banned from life from using pens and pencils. Also, possibly, food, water and oxygen. (*He looks up from the notes, smiles cheerfully at Nutley*) Any questions?

Nutley Oh yes. Lots.

Bill Carry on. I'm here to help.

Nutley Are you genuine?

Bill Yes. I'm the real Bill Robson. Ask anybody. Ask Mrs Scott.

Ellen He is the real Bill Robson.

Nutley But you're not a real poet, are you?

Bill That's not for me to say. I can only do my best as I pass along life's highway, and leave others to judge——

Nutley produces Bill's exercise book full of poems

Nutley I read your poems.

Bill That's nice. You should have picked up some useful tips reading them. It's all good stuff.

Nutley You didn't write them.

Bill Of course I did. That's my handwriting. Ask anybody. Ask (Mrs Scott).

Ellen That's Mr Robson's handwriting. (*She is quick at learning Bill's games*)

Nutley But you stole the poems from other writers.

Bill That's right.

Nutley There isn't an original thought anywhere in this book.

Bill That's not fair. There's a lot of original thoughts. They're just not mine, that's all. They're other people's original thoughts.

Nutley And you got this job as writer-in-residence by fraud and deception.

Bill Obviously.

Nutley You don't deny it?

Bill I had no choice, man. I'm not a proper writer, so if I'm trying to get a job where you're supposed to be a proper writer, well, fraud and deception's my only chance, isn't it?

Nutley turns to Ellen in frustration

Nutley What do you think about it, Mrs Scott?

Ellen About what, Mr Nutley?

Nutley Sharing your office with a liar and a cheat?

Ellen I cannot tell a lie. It's quite good fun. Mr Robson keeps me amused with his chirpy Northumbrian folk tales. The wit and wisdom of the coalface. The most unforgettable coal-miner I've ever forgotten about. It's a bit like sharing an office with the South Shields edition of Reader's Digest. I can think of better things. But I can also think of worse things. More worse things than better things, probably.

Nutley Do you realize all that is also a pack of lies?

Bill Oh howay man, we've had enough packs of lies for one day.

Nutley All the howays in the world do not alter the fact ... that is also a pack of lies.

Ellen Do I take it ... you're now talking about a different pack of lies?

Nutley I am.

Bill Can you let us know which pack of lies you're on about? So I can have my story ready?

Nutley The pack of lies about your being an ex-miner.

Bill I see. That pack of lies.

Nutley It is, isn't it?

Bill I don't give in as easily as that. I want to see the colour of your evidence.

Nutley Evidence. (*He picks up the exercise book*) You made a simple mistake.

Ellen Not the fingerprint on the wine-glass?

Nutley The name and address on your so-called collected poems.

Bill So I didn't lose it. If this book should chance to roam, tear it up and send it home.

Nutley I called at your home on the way here. I spoke to your wife.

Bill Did you like her? She's canny, isn't she? Hey, and I'll tell you what. She makes a wonderful pease pudding. (*He turns to Ellen*) Have you ever had pease pudding?

Ellen No, but I know a poem about it.

Bill You know a poem about everything.

Nutley At the press conference it was stated that you came to London to raise money during the miners' strike. That your pit was closed and you were made redundant. And you then decided to stay in London and try to make your way as a poet and writer.

Bill Well, what's wrong with that? It's a good story.

Nutley What's wrong with it? None of it's true.

Bill Parts of it are true. I'd go as far as to say that most of it's true.

Nutley You didn't move to London after the strike. You moved to London in nineteen seventy-four.

Bill That's right. After the strike.

Nutley But——

Bill The nineteen seventy-four strike.

Ellen Oh, I say, well played, sir. (*She observes the dispute, enjoying it as she might enjoy Wimbledon on television*)

Bill It's just the order got mixed up. I came to London after the nineteen seventy-four strike. I raised money during the last one. And I'm now making my way as a poet and writer. Doing quite well. I'm a writer-in-residence at the moment. So, like I say, most of it's true. It's only the order that people get confused.

Nutley But what about the big lie?

Bill You've spotted a big lie?

Nutley Yes. You were never a coal-miner in your life.

Bill That's true.

Ellen That is quite a big lie, Mr Robson.

Bill But it wasn't my fault.

Ellen Not your fault you were never a coal-miner? I think we deserve an explanation of that.

Bill They closed the pit in the village.

Nutley The village?

Bill It was what we call a pit village. A village with a pit. And they closed the pit.

Nutley Your pit village was a very pleasant, middle-class suburb of Newcastle-upon-Tyne called Gosforth.

Bill Once upon a time, Gosforth was a pit village. Now, all right, I'll grant you, the pit was closed years before I was born. But that's just a historical accident. I could easily have been a coal-miner. And if I'd been a coal-miner, I could easily have been made redundant.

Ellen You've just been unlucky, that's all.

Bill Exactly. (*A beat then:*) And I do come from a mining family.

Nutley Your father was a teacher.

Bill Did wor lass tell you all this?

Nutley I'm sorry. I don't speak vernacular.

Bill Did my wife tell you all this?

Nutley Yes. She's a very delightful woman and deeply attached to the truth.

Bill I know. She's funny like that.

Ellen And is it a good marriage?

Bill Oh ay, I enjoy it.

Ellen And does your wife enjoy the marriage?

Bill I think so. (*He turns to Nutley*) Did you ask her about that?

Nutley I formed the impression that she had a great deal of affection for you.

Bill That's a relief. I'm glad she loves me. The cherry stones were right.

Ellen You've certainly done a very thorough piece of research Mr Nutley.

Nutley Thank you.

Bill Just seems like a nosy parker to me. Nothing personal.

Ellen I can understand why he did it.

Bill Can you? Apart from being a nosy parker?

Ellen Yes. Mr Nutley wanted your job. Is that right?

Bill You wanted to be writer-in-residence?

Nutley Yes. Why not?

Bill No reason. It's a free country. And you didn't make the short list?

Nutley No, I didn't make the short list.

Bill What did you submit? As a sample of your work?

Nutley The two novels about Lorca.

Bill Why, man, you had no chance. They're no good. You'd have been better off copying something out of a book.

Nutley I wouldn't have minded losing to a real writer, but I do mind losing to a con man.

Bill See your point. Bit like Newcastle United losing the Cup Final to the East Midlands formation dancing team.

Ellen You are a little bit of a shit, aren't you?

Bill Me?

Ellen Yes, you.

Bill Don't say you're turning against me, Mrs Scott. After all these years standing shoulder to shoulder on the picket line ...

Ellen As you might say, nothing personal. But I would like to know the truth.

Bill As in the whole and nothing but the ... ?

Ellen nods. She isn't joking

Ellen Yes, please. I don't mind your borrowing a few poems. I don't mind your fooling a selection panel of councillors. Any self-respecting con man should be able to do that. But I *do* mind your pretending to be a miner.

Bill You do?

Ellen Yes.

Bill That's a funny thing to bother about.

Ellen I only bother about it because my father really was a pitman.

Bill Was he? Whereabouts? The North-East?

Ellen In Kent.

Bill Good battlers, the Kent miners. That's canny.

Ellen His entire body was impregnated with coal dust and he coughed himself to death at the age of sixty. It was not canny.

Pause

I think I'm entitled to the whole truth.

Bill You shall have it, comrade. (*He takes a deep breath to summon up some truth then:*) The story so far. Bill Robson, born Gosforth in uptown Newcastle. Left school with three O levels, including an A in technical drawing. Big disappointment to my father.

Ellen Father, who was a teacher, rather than a miner.

Bill A teacher. Not a very good one. Not a very happy one.

Ellen But he wanted you to follow in his footsteps?

Bill He didn't leave any. That's the sadness. You couldn't see where he'd been.

Ellen Yes, that's a sadness.

Bill So. I came to London to seek my fortune.

Nutley After the strike in nineteen seventy-four.

Bill More or less. Not exactly the day after but sort of approximately around that time, roughly.

Nutley, in the interests of his highly personal research, makes notes of everything. He seems to do this throughout his life

Ellen And did you find it?

Bill What?

Ellen Your fortune. You came to London to seek it.

Bill No. Mind you, I didn't really want a fortune. Not in money. What I wanted was ... (*He hesitates, trying to define in his head what it was he wanted. He finds a road out of the thicket and continues:*) When you two went to school, did either of you have Social Studies? Or Liberal Education? That sort of stuff?

Ellen Mostly we had trigonometry and Thomas Hardy, with a little elementary basket-weaving for light relief.

Nutley We did Social Skills.

Bill Which knife and fork to use, like?

Nutley And spoons at A level. (*He smiles at his own joke*)

Bill Spoons at A level. That's good. Should I tell him about Jimmy James and the lion? We could work him into the act. Would you like to be Eli?

Ellen I want to know about your liberal education, and where it went wrong. Mr Nutley can be Eli another time.

Bill All right. We had this feller, see. Mr Barras. Taught Social Studies and Liberal Education. Sometimes both, on the same day. Brilliant feller. He had lots of good ideas. They had to get rid of him in the end, that's how good he was. And he used to tell us about job satisfaction.

Ellen That old thing.

Bill He'd say ... "Everybody can't be a concert pianist or a television newsreader, but there's no reason why you kids" ... meaning us ... "shouldn't all find something to do that gives you job satisfaction."

Ellen You believed him?

Bill Certainly I believed him. When you're fifteen you'll believe anything, if it's what you want to hear.

Nutley Therefore, what you were seeking in London was not your fortune, but job satisfaction?

Bill That's right. I mean, there was no way I was going to find it on Tyneside. They were closing three shipyards every week.

Ellen And the pit was closed years before you were born.

Bill So there wasn't a lot of satisfaction around the place.

Ellen Was there any in London?

Bill There were jobs. So that gave us a head start. I thought I'd keep on trying jobs until I found one with some satisfaction.

Nutley What sort of jobs were these? (*He's still cross-examining and making notes*)

Bill Mostly ... serfdom.

Ellen Working in the paddyfields? Rotating your crops?

Bill That's the principle of it. I started as a hotel porter. Then I got lateral promotion as a barman. Then I became a waiter.

Ellen In the hotel?

Bill That's where I started. Then I moved around. I've done the lot. Restaurants, bistros, trattorias, French, Italian, Chinese, Indian ...

Ellen Forgive my being personal, but did you change your accent?

Bill Definitely not. I laid it on stronger. I am here to tell you, Mrs Scott, there is no job satisfaction in running backwards and forwards across crowded rooms carrying trays full of *moules marinière* and *scampi provençale*. I had to make my own satisfaction.

Ellen By dropping the tray?

Bill By telling lies.

Ellen About yourself? About the scampi?

Bill About everything. But mostly about myself.

Ellen A terribly amusing waiter gets better tips?

Bill He does. But that's not the important thing. The important thing is to stop being invisible. It's not much fun being invisible. You're certainly not invisible if you're the only waiter in the West End who's an ex-pitman with a false leg.

Nutley False, as in artificial?

Bill Yes. It's not a thing I like to talk about, but I lost my leg in a pit accident, that's why I became a waiter, I didn't realize the limp was that obvious . . . (*He demonstrates the limp*)

Ellen That's a very impressive limp.

Bill I got really good at limping. It's quite hard, you know, doing a good limp when there's nothing wrong with you. And I worked on the dialogue as well. Helping them with the menu and the wine list. The noble Geordie savage speaks. "Yes, sir, I can heartily recommend the *sole bon femme*, it's made to a traditional peasant recipe very popular in parts of West Hartlepool." "Yes, madam, you'll find the Chardonnay a very amusing wine, sharp on the palate, good for the complexion and guaranteed to give you naughty ideas in the early hours of the morning." (*He pauses, pleased with the quality of his recollections*) It was all a load of crap, but if you say it with a broad Geordie accent, and remember the limp, you're away. After a bit I stopped calling people sir and madam. I called them all hinny and pet. They loved it. They'd come in and demand to be on my table. (*Posh voice*) "We want to be served by our canny Geordie pitman."

Ellen You'd reached the top of your profession. I'd call that job satisfaction.

Nutley I'm sure Mr Baras would have been proud of you.

Bill I got so good at it, I didn't have to think about it any more. And I started listening. To the customers. I made a great discovery. *They* were all telling lies as well. Bigger lies than mine. (*Telling the stories, he reproduces the voices*) Businessmen saying . . . "Yes, it's all settled, we just need two more signatures" . . . Media people . . . "Yes, I read the book, I absolutely adored it" . . . Middle-aged lovers straight out of *Brief Encounter* . . . "Darling, I promise to tell her next week, and I've already spoken to my solicitor . . ."

Ellen We know about those lies. We live with them. (*She offers an example*) I'm sorry about the delay in delivery but there's been a fire at the factory.

Nutley The cheque's in the post.

Ellen I tried to ring you all day Sunday but all I got was the engaged signal.

Nutley We have read your manuscript with great interest.

Ellen There's nothing organically wrong.

Nutley I love you.

A brief sense that Nutley has given away more than he intended. They respect his privacy and don't pursue it

Bill Any road, it was hearing the customers telling lies that made up my mind for me. I asked for my cards.

Ellen They tell lies. You tell lies. What's the difference?

Bill The difference is they told lies and they could afford to eat there. Sixty quid for two excluding wine. I could only afford to work there. It didn't make sense.

Nutley And your duty lay elsewhere.

Bill Did it? (*He hadn't realized that*)

Nutley Obviously.

Ellen Really? (*She's baffled too*)

Nutley Society is driven by the market forces. They teach it in schools. It's replaced Liberal Education and Social Skills. The new commandment: thou shalt maximize the commercial possibilities of thine assets. A liar of Mr Robson's quality should be working in advertising or public relations or politics.

Bill Is that what Lorca would have done?

Nutley No. He would have done the exact opposite.

Bill And look what happened to him.

Ellen There are still a few thousand things I don't understand, Inspector.

Bill A few thousand? That's not many.

Ellen One minute you're everybody's favourite waiter. Working-class hero. Mr Personality himself. Then you see the error of everybody's ways. A dark light on the road out of Damascus. You decide: Bill Robson will be redeemed, before it's too late. Is that the picture?

Bill Yes. And very nicely put.

Ellen I read lots of books.

Bill I knew there must be a reason.

Ellen It's quite a big leap from disenchanted waiter to writer-in-residence.

Bill It was something else Mr Barras used to say.

Nutley Mr Barras has a great deal to answer for.

Bill He said a writer's job was to tell the truth.

Nutley Obviously.

Bill It wasn't obvious to me.

Ellen It isn't obvious to all writers but who am I to argue with Mr Barrass?

Bill Never mind. I thought if I could get this job I'd have three months surrounded by books. All of them full of truth. I might acquire the taste. Get to like it.

Nutley But you told lies to get the job.

Bill It was the only way I could get the job.

Ellen How many books have you read while you've been here?

Sharp reaction from Bill

Bill How many?

Ellen In your restless pursuit of truth?

Bill You mean all the way through? Cover to cover?

Ellen That's the recommended way of reading a book.

Bill does a quick count on his fingers then announces the result

Bill None.

Nutley You read my books.

Bill Oh yes, I read your books, Mr Nutley. That's how I was able to give you my critical assessment. (*Bill looks at Ellen implying: don't give me away*)

Ellen But excluding Mr Nutley's manuscripts which, as we know, you read with great care and diligence, you haven't read any others.

Bill Books . . . of the sort that stand on your shelves . . . no, I haven't. Not as such.

Ellen So your quest for truth is also a lie?

Bill I told you on the first day that I was feckless.

Ellen I thought you were lying.

Bill You still think I'm . . . a little bit of a shit?

Ellen Yes, I do. Truly.

There is the sound of the outside door. Ellen sees a customer come into the library

Ellen Customer. Your turn to be on the picket line.

Bill We'll set aside our differences for the greater good.

Bill exits

Nutley starts to pack away his Lorca manuscript in its box. A casual aside to Ellen

Nutley Did you have a chance to read this, Mrs Scott?

Ellen plays for time, pretending not to have understood

Ellen I'm sorry. Did I read what?

Nutley Did you read my manuscript?

Bill appears in the doorway and overhears the next bit

Ellen I browsed a little. Not enough to form any real critical judgement.

Bill (*quietly*) And the cock crowed a third time.

Ellen (*also quietly*) Swine!

Bill raises his voice, slightly louder than normal, to announce

Bill Councillor Graham, Deputy-Co-Chair-Person of the Libraries Sub-Committee.

Graham enters, looking a little hassled

Graham Good-afternoon, Mrs Scott, good-afternoon, Mr——(*She knows she knows Nutley but can't remember his name*)

Nutley Nutley.

Graham Mr Nutley.

Ellen Good-afternoon, Councillor. What can we do for you?

Graham That remains to be seen. I came as soon as I got the phone call.

Ellen Did we telephone? I certainly didn't. Did you? (*She asks Bill*)

Bill No. I didn't telephone. Did you?

He asks Nutley, who is baffled

Nutley Pardon?

Graham I was telephoned by a Mrs Dickenson.
Ellen Mrs Dickenson?
Bill Mrs Dickenson as in deaf old Mrs Dickenson?
Graham She sounded quite old. And I had to raise my voice to make myself understood.
Ellen Good. We're all talking about the same person.
Graham She rang to say you were on strike.
Ellen Correct.
Graham Apparently, you denied her Barbara Cartland.
Ellen Not me personally. Mr Robson denied her Barbara Cartland.

Graham turns to Bill

Bill It's true. Mind you, I wasn't picking on Barbara Cartland. I'd have taken the same attitude if it had been Shakespeare himself. It was purely deaf old Mrs Dickenson we were picking on.
Graham What *is* going on?
Ellen A strike is going on.
Bill And it's a well-known fact that strike action only becomes effective when it hits the elderly and the disabled. We're really quite lucky that Mrs Dickenson came in, 'cause that way we get two for the price of one.
Graham Am I permitted to know what the strike is about?
Bill Obviously. It's about branch library closures.
Ellen We're against them.
Bill And we're against hit lists.
Ellen Especially if we're on them.
Bill We're also against supermarkets.
Ellen In fact, it's true to say we're against practically everything.
Bill It's the only way to be.
Nutley If I may observe, as a regular library user, I'm against everything mentioned so far.
Bill Everybody is ranged against you, Councillor. The rank and file.
Nutley The creative artists.
Bill And the sick and the elderly.
Ellen Which just about makes it unanimous.
Graham Apart from the Libraries Sub-Committee.

Pause

Ellen I knew there was somebody we'd overlooked.
Bill I still think there's room for negotiation.
Graham We can't negotiate under duress.
Bill Duress? You call this duress? You're talking to an ex-pitman.
Ellen (*gently*) More or less.
Bill (*ignoring her*) I'll tell you this for nothing, Councillor, we've got duress we haven't even used yet.

Nutley picks up his box

Nutley I'll leave you to your negotiations.
Bill You stay here, Mr Nutley.

Nutley I've indicated my support in principle and——

Bill (*breaking in*) We need you to help with the duress.

Nutley Do you?

Ellen Do we?

Bill You bet.

Nutley (*shrugging*) All right. (*He puts his box down*)

Graham Are we going to discuss this calmly and sensibly?

Bill We're happy to. We can't speak for the other side.

Graham Can we clarify the issues?

Bill There's only one issue. You want to close the library and we want it to stay open. We're on strike and we'll stay on strike till you and your committee change your mind.

Graham Is that your view, Mrs Scott?

Bill Watch it. She's trying to divide and rule.

Ellen That is my view, Councillor.

Graham But I explained the situation fully this morning. Nothing has changed since then.

Bill Wrong. A lot of things have changed.

Graham Have they?

Ellen Have they?

Bill We've had a sudden outburst of truth. Your credibility is at stake.

Graham I can't see why.

Bill I'm told credibility is very important for a politician. It doesn't matter what lies you tell as long as you don't get caught out. Bit like life, really ...

Graham (*turning to Ellen*) Mrs Scott, do you have the remotest idea what Mr Robson is talking about?

Ellen I have a remote idea, yes. But don't worry. You'll find the more he explains, the less you'll understand.

Bill switches his attention to Nutley

Bill Mr Nutley. Show Councillor Graham your notebook.

Nutley My notebook?

Bill Show her your notebook.

Nutley Why?

Bill Just do it, there's a good lad.

Ellen Show her your notebook. (*Ellen just wants to find out what the hell this is all about*)

Nutley checks through his pockets and eventually finds his notebook

Nutley My notebook.

Graham A very nice notebook.

Bill It's all in that notebook.

Graham What is?

Bill Your credibility. Your committee's credibility. The Council's credibility. Democracy's credibility.

Ellen Well, it is quite a slim notebook.

Bill In that notebook, there's a story. How your Council was fooled by an imposter. How you have given public money to a confidence trickster.
Graham Who exactly are you talking about?
Bill Me exactly.

Ellen has now grasped the game plan

Ellen You appointed Mr Robson as writer-in-residence even though he's never written a word in his life.
Graham But we read your poems.
Bill Other people's poems, pet.
Ellen Stolen from other people's books. (*Aside to Bill*) I don't think she's a hamster.
Bill Remains to be seen.

Now Nutley decides to join in

Nutley I imagine there was a deal of sympathy on the selection committee, since Mr Robson claimed to be an ex-miner.
Graham To an extent. Certainly on the left and . . . er . . . centre left . . . (*As she decides where she belongs*)
Bill And the right didn't turn up on the day. He was busy in the City.
Graham So we appointed a man who isn't a genuine writer and there was an element of sympathy because of his mining background . . .
Bill I've never been down a pit in my life, Councillor.
Graham Never?
Bill Pack of lies.
Graham That's much worse than lying about your alleged poetry.
Bill That's what they said.
Ellen We were truly appalled.
Nutley Disgusted.
Bill Especially as Mr Nutley applied for the job and didn't get it. That's why he's written it all down in his little book.
Nutley It seemed the obvious thing to do. A verbatim record of the evidence.
Bill And I haven't even told them about going to prison.
Ellen You've been in prison?
Bill I was well-behaved. I got full remission.

Nutley starts writing in his book

Nutley What was the charge?
Bill No charge. It was free.
Graham When was this, Mr Robson?
Bill I'm saying no more. I've paid my debt to society. The slate is wiped clean.
Nutley Presumably it's all on the public record?
Bill If you know where to look.
Ellen I assume this wasn't for a crime of violence.
Bill Certainly not. I'm too small for violence. It was more in the area of petty fraud, false pretences. That's always been my speciality.

Ellen Robbing the rich to feed the poor?
Bill Robbing the rich and keeping it.
Nutley Where should I look?
Bill Sorry, kiddar, don't know what you're on about.
Nutley Whereabouts in the public record?
Bill Usual places. Mind you, all this was under my other name. One of my other names.
Ellen How many names do you have?
Bill I'd rather not say. It's a sensible precaution when you've got more than one wife, don't you think?

Nutley writes that down, damn quick

Ellen The Marriage Guidance Council recommends it, I believe.
Graham Very well. We've now established you're a liar, and a bigamist, and an ex-criminal.
Bill But I'm canny with it, mind.
Graham How does all this relate to the strike?
Ellen (*taking up the running*) I can explain that.
Graham Please do, Mrs Scott.
Ellen Mr Nutley, in addition to being a novelist of considerable potential, is, as we all know, a free-lance journalist. He has kept a careful record of everything that has been said. (*Ellen looks at Nutley for confirmation*) Correct?
Nutley Correct.

And then she checks with Bill

Ellen Correct?
Bill Right on the nose.

Now they all three know where they're heading. Ellen crosses to the telephone

Ellen One telephone call to Fleet Street ...
Nutley Or even Wapping ...

They pause, wonder briefly about Wapping

Bill Esther Rantzen?
Ellen Wherever.
Nutley It's a perfect story. We have left-wing loonies ... (*He browses through the pages of the notebook*)
Bill Absentee right-wing loonies ...
Ellen And ever-present middle-of-the-road loonies.

The sound of the outside door. Bill sees a customer

Bill A customer.
Ellen (*checking*) Not only that. A senior citizen. A very old customer.
Bill In pebble glasses. He must be almost blind.
Ellen (*nodding*) Calls in once a week for his large print Molly Parkin.
Bill No wonder he needs pebble glasses. (*He crosses to the door*) I'll give him

a bit of duress. (*To Graham*) Moral. When a canny little Geordie walks through the door, run for your life.

Bill exits

A Lighting change. A little music over: let's say a reprise of "Dance to thi Daddy.". Minimal set change to leave us with the display screen and three chairs forming the local authority's Press Conference kit. Which means we're ready for:

SCENE 2

In effect, the same situation as at the play's opening, except that Graham is now flanked by Ellen and Nutley

Another shuffling silence then:

Graham Do you think we should start?
Ellen Well, we are ten minutes late already.
Graham I shall never come to terms with media apathy.
Ellen You circulated the usual suspects?
Graham Yes.
Nutley Why don't you simply grasp the nettle, Councillor Graham?
Graham Why not indeed? (*She addresses the audience, clutching her clipboard like a comfort blanket*) Good-morning, and welcome to the Civic Centre Annexe, for this press conference. My name is Councillor Graham Deputy-Co-Chair-Person of the Libraries Sub-Committee. I have to record apologies from my fellow-Deputy-Co-Chairs. Councillor Bradley-Willis of the Conservative group has been unavoidably detained in the City . . .
Ellen Assisting the police with their inquiries?
Graham No, I don't think so.
Ellen Forgive me, Councillor, a modest and unworthy jest.
Nutley Not according to my information.

Graham battles on gamely. Her sole aim is to get the whole thing over as soon as possible

Graham And Councillor Baxter of the Labour Group has a sudden crisis on his university campus.
Nutley He's probably been asked to do some teaching.
Ellen Another modest and unworthy jest?
Graham Pass. (*She checks her notes and continues*) I have agreed to take responsibility for an official announcement concerning our Eastwood Road branch. Contrary to rumours and press speculation, this branch is not, repeat not, to be closed. Tentative discussions did take place and an informal feasibility study was commissioned, but following a free and frank exchange of view with the staff at the library, it became clear that

closure would not be in the best interests of the community. (*She turns to Ellen*) Would you like to say anything, Mrs Scott?

Ellen Yes. I would like to place on record my appreciation of the open-minded spirit with which Councillor Graham listened to our views on the subject of the library's future. The decision to keep the library open is majestic in its statesmanship. And statesmanlike in its majesty.

Graham Thank you, Mrs Scott. Perhaps you'd like to deal with the next item yourself?

Ellen Thank you. Now, you may remember that the previous press conference we held was to announce the appointment of our new writer-in-residence. On the other hand, since none of you attended that day, you probably don't remember. At any rate, on that day, we announced the appointment of Mr William Robson, a fine and talented Tyneside poet, as writer-in-residence at Eastwood Road. Unfortunately, for personal reasons he has now had to resign his position. I know something of the circumstances and you must take my word that his every action has proved him to be . . . a very gallant gentleman.

Nutley I agree.

Graham hesitates, then decides she might as well agree, too

Graham Yes, I agree. As well.

Ellen In his place, our good friend Mr Gerald Nutley, here on the platform with us, will be starting work from tomorrow which is, as you might guess, why he is on the platform with us. Mr Nutley is a novelist, currently working on a trilogy about Federico García Lorca.

Nutley preens a little

Nutley I'd be very happy to answer any questions about my work.

Ellen Quite so.

Graham We have made special arrangements for questions. Later.

Ellen One more important point about Mr Nutley's position as writer-in-residence. He will not, in fact, be in residence. For two reasons. First, the back room at Eastwood Road simply isn't large enough for two people to work efficiently. I believe the Libraries Sub-Committee is looking into the possibility of building us an extension . . . (*With an expectant look at Graham*)

Graham (*responding*) We have appointed a sub-committee which has a mandate to set up a working party.

Ellen Secondly, Councillor Graham felt and I must say I agree, that Mr Nutley's talent and expertise should really be exploited outside, in the community, at street level and, no disrespect, as far away from my office as possible. (*A nice smile to sweeten the insult*)

Graham Thank you, Mrs Scott. (*She turns to the audience*) That concludes the formal announcements. Everything we've told you is fully detailed in your press pack . . .

Probably all three of them hold up copies of this: a simple cardboard folder bearing the local authority logo and containing a couple of pages of neatly typed, photocopied bullshit

Nutley Any questions about Lorca? (*He's keen to answer some questions*)
Graham May I explain our new arrangements regarding questions.

Hereabouts Bernard enters. He's holding one end of a measuring tape, which stretches taut across the stage behind the three speakers. By implication somebody is holding the other end. We don't see who it is

It has been pointed out to us that one possible explanation for the variable attendance at our press conferences is the lack of . . . er, liquid refreshment.

Bernard calls to his off-stage colleague

Bernard Twenty-five feet seven inches.

Reactions from the three onstage. They pretend nothing has happened

Graham And to be sure, the promise of . . . er, liquid refreshment seems to have boosted the attendance today. All that being so, you are cordially invited to ask your questions of any of us, informally . . .

Bernard has been staring at his measuring tape, trying to figure something out. He reaches a conclusion

Bernard Sorry. That's in metres. Twenty-five feet seven inches. But in metres.

Graham soldiers on: it's almost over now

Graham I suggest we adjourn to Sub-Committee Room nine-B for indepth questioning, plus a little white wine and some cheesy nibbles . . .

Their reactions imply that the press corps is up, away and out of the door on the word "wine"

Ellen How many bottles of wine?
Graham Two.
Ellen We're probably too late already.

Nutley and Graham get up and exit

As Ellen crosses with Bernard, she recognizes him

Bernard, isn't it?
Bernard Yes. Sort of.
Ellen Is the Civic Centre Annexe about to become a supermarket?
Bernard I'm just measuring up the room.
Ellen Metrically or imperially?
Bernard I expect so.

Graham enters

Graham Mrs Scott . . . are you any good with a cork-screw?
Ellen Well, I've read a lot of books.

Graham exits

(*Turning to Bernard*) I wish you joy of your dimensions.

Ellen exits

Whereupon Bill enters from the opposite side holding the other end of the tape, plus a clipboard. He is in charge of the survey. Bernard is his lackey

Bill Listen, kiddar. We need to reach an understanding if we're going to work together.

Bernard What for?

Bill We need to agree whether we're doing our survey in metres or in feet and inches.

Bernard That's all right by me. Let's agree.

Bill What normally happens in Mr Carruthers' department?

Bernard Normally, well, we reckon a bit of each, sort of thing. (*He shows Bill the tape*) Trouble is, you get feet and inches on one side of the tape and metres on the other. It's dead easy to get them mixed up.

Bill I'm sure.

Bernard What did you do when you were an architect?

Bill Feet and inches. But we're very old-fashioned in the ancient Kingdom of Northumbria.

Bernard I've noticed that.

Bill (*giving the place a casual once-over*) It'll make a canny supermarket though.

Bernard Are you really a qualified architect?

Bill To some extent.

Bernard So what were you doing working in the library?

Bill That was a sideways career move into poetry and literature.

Bernard It looked a doddle to me.

Bill Isn't this a doddle?

Bernard There's a lot of standing up and walking about. Sometimes out of doors.

Bill Fresh air brings on your cough, does it?

Bernard Libraries are all indoors and sitting down.

Bill I found I could handle the sitting down. It was the poetry and literature gave me trouble.

Bernard Just words, isn't it?

Bill So they tell me.

Bernard (*looking off-stage*) There's white wine and cheesy nibbles in Room nine-B.

Bill You can't blame a room for what happens inside it.

Bernard Do you think they allow gatecrashers?

Bill There'd have to be a special meeting of the sub-committee to decide that.

Bernard We could go in and measure it.

Bill looks at the plan on his clipboard

Bill We haven't been asked to measure Room nine-B.

Bernard So we'll give them something extra, on top, won't we? No extra charge. And we'll probably score for wine.

Bill You're a wine expert?

Bernard I like anything that makes me pissed.

Bill With proper training, I could turn you into a really good Geordie.

Bernard No thanks. Don't really want to be anything.

Bill That's what I like. A young man with ambition.

A beat then:

Howay then. Let's try the Château de Sub-Committee.

They exit

Lighting change. Music over: Miles Davis playing "U 'n' I". A chirpy link to:

SCENE 3

The library. It's a month later or thereabouts. It's also first thing in the morning

Ellen comes in carrying the morning mail. She drops it on her desk while she hangs up her coat, fills the kettle and switches it on, ready for her early morning tea-break

She sits down at her desk and starts to open letters. She reads the first, and more or less simultaneously dials a number on the phone. By the time the person at the other end has replied she's ripped open a couple more too. She speaks

Ellen Good-morning Mr Nutley, how are you? . . . And the floppy discs? . . . Good. Do you have your diary to hand? A couple of dates for you . . . a week on Wednesday, seven o'clock in the evening, the Church of the Beloved Saviour Youth Club would like you to speak to their members . . . I think you're a carefully planned alternative to table tennis. . . . Yes, I'm sure they'd love to hear about Lorca. And a week on Friday . . . two o'clock in the afternoon . . . could you go to the Darby and Joan Club? . . . What? . . . (*She checks the letter*) Well, they don't say they *don't* want to hear about Lorca, so why not hit them with a couple of hours of old Federico García? I'm sure they'll love it. I'll ring tomorrow if there are more sweet surprises. 'Bye. (*She carries on checking through the letters. She arrives at one that stops her in her tracks*) Good heavens. (*She reads aloud*) "Dear Mrs Scott . . ."

Bill steps onstage, but not in the scene

Bill Dear Mrs Scott . . .

We move out of naturalistic mode, perhaps with a modest lighting change, but nothing fancy and fey. In the first part of this sequence, essentially she's hearing the letter in his voice, and adding her comments

Ellen A sweet surprise.

Bill I don't suppose you expected to hear from me but I owe you a few explanations and apologies.

Ellen Yes. Running into double figures.

Bill But the first thing you'll notice is the postmark on the envelope.

Ellen (*checking*) Noted.

Bill Yes, I've moved back to canny Newcastle. It hasn't changed all that much. We've got too many supermarkets, but you can't destroy the old traditions ... the crowds of people down at the dole, and the tomcats walking in twos along the Scotswood Road.

Ellen Whatever that means.

Bill Now for some explanations and apologies. I told you a lot of lies when I was at the library. I even told you lies about the lies. It would take too long to explain them all properly but I think you should know that I've never been to prison, and I've never been a waiter, and I've never worked in a hotel. Also, Mr Carruthers, the borough surveyor, was a bit snotty about my architectural qualifications. He said an O level in technical drawing and a school trip to Durham Cathedral didn't add up to an architectural qualification.

Ellen Intolerant swine.

Bill I tried to explain ... it depends how you look at these things. But somehow borough surveyors are more set in their ways of thinking than most people I meet. Not that I've met that many borough surveyors. In the end, it seemed like a sideways career move back to Tyneside was the best bet. I needed time to think and everybody up here's got plenty of time for thinking.

Ellen starts writing a replay as Bill continues speaking his letter

I've been thinking a lot about work, and about job satisfaction ... that thing Mr Barras taught me about in school. I look at you, and I see a contented woman. Your job fits you, like a suit of clothes. Then I look at young Bernard. He doesn't see any point in anything. Then I look at me. Somewhere there's a suit of clothes to fit me, but I'm buggered if I can find it. Should I worry about this? I don't want to be invisible. But I don't want to be dead, and young Bernard might as well be. That's if you think work matters.

Ellen Dear Mr Robson.

Now she reads her letter and Bill comments on it

Bill That's canny. I never expected a reply.

Ellen Correct. I was very surprised to receive your letter. Also delighted. That is ... I *think* I was delighted.

Bill Oh, howay lass, you mean you're not sure?

Ellen It was great fun having you working in the library but you have an unfortunate knack of leaning heavily on everybody's jugular vein.

Bill Sorry pet. Not a hamster. Sorry, Mrs Scott.

Ellen You see, I was brought up to believe in truth. I was educated to believe in truth. I don't know whether you've heard of George Bernard Shaw?

Bill Heard of him? I saw him play against Newcastle United.

Ellen He said ... "I believe ... in the might of design, the mystery of colour, the redemption of all things by Beauty everlasting, and the message of Art that has made these hands blessed."

Bill Ye bugger. That's nice.

Ellen In the end, that's all I believe. Art and Beauty and Truth are the only things that matter a damn. I try to put it into practice working in a tatty little branch library patronized by deaf old women and short-sighted old men. And when my little palace of truth was under threat, how did we save it? By telling a pack of lies. That worries the hell out of me. *You* worry the hell out of me.

Bill smiles and replies

Bill Dear Mrs Scott. Don't worry about a thing. Certainly don't worry about me, I'm not worth it. But here's your answer. Telling lies is all right, subject to certain conditions. First, you shouldn't hurt anybody.

Ellen Agreed.

Bill Second, it should only be in a good cause.

Ellen Agreed.

Bill Third, you should only do it to people in authority, like politicians and their time-serving lackeys.

Ellen Principalities ...

Bill Or politicians ...

Ellen And powers ...

Bill Or politicians. We'll have to keep on telling lies to politicians until we get control of our lives. Then we'll be our own politicians, and we won't have to tell lies any more. For the moment, they are the enemy.

Ellen They killed my father.

Bill They killed your father.

Ellen And they deprived you of a proper suit of clothes.

Bill Fourth principle of telling lies. The people who matter ... the people I love and who love me ... they know bonny well when I'm telling lies. Those who can't tell, why, they're not worth bothering with.

Ellen The Tyneside air seems to be agreeing with you.

Bill It's a magic blend of brown ale fumes and Woodbine smoke and long memories. And I'll tell you something else, Mrs Scott.

Ellen Another surprise?

Bill Another surprise. I've made a sideways career move. I've decided to become a poet.

Ellen A poet?

Bill I've written my first bit ... it's not a whole poem ... I think they call it a fragment in the trade. I met a canny lad in the *Crown Posada* ... that's a pub on the Newcastle quayside ... and he reckons the great poets wrote loads of fragments ... so I've written my first fragment. Please find enclosed.

Ellen takes the piece of paper bearing Bill's fragment from the envelope. Bill has an identical sheet. They read alternate lines

Bill   Is it so small a thing
Ellen   To have enjoyed the sun,
Bill   To have lived light in the spring,
Ellen   To have loved, to have thought, to have done;
Bill   To have advanced true friends, and beat down baffling foes?

A silence. Then Ellen turns to Bill. They face each other across a distance

Ellen Mr Robson.
Bill Mrs Scott?
Ellen (*holding up the fragment*) Your fragment. Written by Matthew Arnold, eighteen twenty-two to eighteen eighty-eight.
Bill You noticed.

Ellen nods

Ellen I thought I heard a rustling.

Bill shrugs and smiles

BLACK-OUT

FURNITURE AND PROPERTY LIST

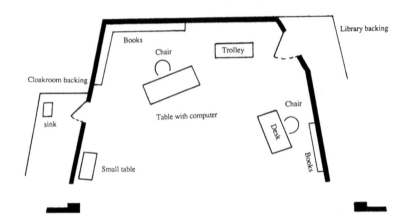

ACT I

SCENE 1

On stage: Display screen. *On it:* authority's logo and slogan
3 chairs

Off stage: File with press release and other papers **(Graham)**
Folder containing exercise book of poems **(Bill)**

SCENE 2

On stage: Table. *On it:* computer keyboard and screen
Trolley. *On it:* books. *By it:* shopping bag containing Bill's exercise book
Cupboards
Shelves. *On them:* books
Desk. *On it:* telephone, papers, pens
3 chairs
Stacks of books
Small table. *On it:* electric kettle (practical), teapot, tea, mugs, milk, sugar, teaspoons
Hooks on wall. *On them:* **Bill's** cap, **Ellen's** coat
In small cloakroom off: practical sink and taps

Off stage: Cardboard box containing two manuscripts **(Nutley)**

Personal: **Bill:** *Sporting Life* in pocket

SCENE 3

On stage: As SCENE 2

Set: **Nutley**'s manuscripts, notepad on desk
Box by desk

Off stage: Clipboard, pencils, measuring tape **(Bernard)**

Personal: **Graham:** wrist-watch

ACT II

SCENE 1

On stage: As SCENE 2

Set: Manuscripts and Ellen's notes in box

Personal: **Nutley:** Bill's exercise book, notebook, pen in pocket

SCENE 2

On stage: As ACT I SCENE 1

Set: Clipboard for **Graham**
Press packs for **Graham**, **Nutley** and **Ellen**

Off stage: One end of measuring tape **(Bernard)**
Other end of measuring tape, clipboard, pen **(Bill)**

SCENE 3

On stage: As ACT I SCENE 2

Strike: Box with manuscripts, notebook
Bill's cap, **Ellen**'s coat from hooks

Set: Writing paper on desk

Off stage: Letters including one from Bill with poem fragment **(Ellen)**
Sheet of paper with poem fragment **(Bill)**

LIGHTING PLOT

Property fittings required: nil

2 interiors

ACT I, SCENE 1. Morning

To open: General lighting

Cue 1   **Bill:** "... really be in residence."   (Page 4)
           Fade lighting to cover scene change

ACT I, SCENE 2. Morning

To open: General lighting

Cue 2   **Bill:** "... the inside story."   (Page 15)
           Fade to Black-out

ACT I, SCENE 3. Morning

To open: General lighting

Cue 3   **Bernard** shrugs and carries on   (Page 26)
           Slowly fade to Black-out

ACT II, SCENE 1. Afternoon

To open: General lighting

Cue 4   **Bill** exits   (Page 44)
           Slowly fade lighting to cover scene change

ACT II, SCENE 2. Morning

Cue 5   **Bill** and **Bernard** exit   (Page 48)
           Fade lighting to cover scene change

ACT II, SCENE 3. Morning

To open: General lighting

Cue 6   **Ellen** (*reading aloud*): "Dear Mrs Scott ..."   (Page 48)
           Modest lighting change

Cue 7   **Bill** shrugs and smiles   (Page 51)
           Black-out

EFFECTS PLOT

ACT I

Cue 1   **Bill:** "... really be in residence."   (Page 4)
Music to cover scene change, e.g. "Dance to thi Daddy"

Cue 2   When music ready for SCENE 2   (Page 4)
Fade music

Cue 3   **Ellen:** "... on the word, Mr Robson."   (Page 9)
Outer door opens then closes, off

Cue 4   **Bill:** "I enjoy talking ..."   (Page 13)
Repeat Cue 3

Cue 5   **Nutley** exits   (Page 14)
Pause, then outer door opens then closes, off

Cue 6   **Bill:** "... The inside story."   (Page 15)
Music: Miles Davis/Gil Evans "Sketches of Spain"

Cue 7   As Lights come up on SCENE 3   (Page 16)
Fade music

Cue 8   **Bill:** "... for a bollocking."   (Page 18)
Repeat Cue 3

Cue 9   **Ellen:** "... from food, water and oxygen."   (Page 20)
Telephone rings

Cue 10   **Bernard:** "... hanging's too good for them."   (Page 22)
Repeat Cue 3

Cue 11   **Graham** exits   (Page 25)
Repeat Cue 5

ACT II

Cue 12   As SCENE 1 opens   (Page 27)
Music: Miles Davis "Star People"—fade after a few minutes

Cue 13   **Ellen:** "... we need customers."   (Page 27)
Sound of outer door opening then closing; footsteps

Cue 14   **Bill** returns   (Page 27)
Repeat Cue 3

Cue 15   **Bill:** "What?"   (Page 29)
Repeat Cue 3

Cue 16   **Ellen:** "Yes I do. Truly."   (Page 39)
Repeat Cue 3

Cue 17   **Ellen:** "... middle-of-the-road loonies."   (Page 43)
            Repeat Cue 3

Cue 18   **Bill** exits   (Page 44)
            Music: "Dance to thi Daddy"

Cue 19   When ready for SCENE 2   (Page 44)
            Fade music

Cue 20   **Bill** and **Bernard** exit   (Page 48)
            Music: Miles Davis "U 'n' I"

Cue 21   When ready for SCENE 3   (Page 48)
            Fade music